# ENERGY

Get it
Guard it
Give it

# ENERGY

Lisa O'Neill

MACMILLAN

*For Mikayla, my friend and business manager,*
*who contributes to my energy every day!*
*Thank you for being the best right-hand woman in the world.*

First published in 2024 by Major Street Publishing Pty Ltd

First published in India 2026 by Macmillan
an imprint of Pan Macmillan Publishing India Private Limited
707 Kailash Building
26 K. G. Marg, New Delhi 110001
www.panmacmillan.co.in

Pan Macmillan, The Smithson, 6 Briset Street, Farringdon, London EC1M 5NR
Associated companies throughout the world
www.panmacmillan.com

ISBN 978-93-6113-266-7



1 3 5 7 9 8 6 4 2

Internal design by Production Works
Printed and bound in India by Thomson Press India Ltd.

FSC www.fsc.org
MIX
Paper | Supporting responsible forestry
FSC® C010615

# CONTENTS

1

Introducing Energy 1

2

Physical Energy 13

3

Emotional Energy 45

4

Mental Energy 91

5

Spiritual Energy 127

Appendix: The Seven Chakras 161

About the Author 169

References 171

Recommended Reading List 177

Contact Lisa 181

# 1

# INTRODUCING ENERGY

*'Everything is energy, and that is all there is to it!'*

All we are is energy. Energy is the essence of our existence. We are all energetic beings, and understanding the dynamics of energy is the key to unlocking our true potential. Our energy is transferable and absorbable. Our thoughts begin it, our emotions amplify it and our actions increase or decrease it. Energy is required for growth, change and movement. Energy cannot be seen, but the results of using energy can.

This book is about maximising our life force, about taking responsibility for our energy. It's a call to arms for people who want more energy, who need awareness, attention and action to manage their precious force in the world. We need to become aware of all of the areas where we get energy – the physical, emotional, mental and spiritual. It's literally everything!

Our energy is a decision. We get to decide. We can decide to be happy, to be tired, to be negative, to be grumpy!

We also need to be aware of what depletes our energy. We need to address our energetic plumbing – the blockages, the drains and the leaks! I constantly hear people complaining about how they don't have enough energy and that they wish they had more, but I don't see many people proactively seeking a solution.

So many people are unaware, are living unintentionally and are unhappy. They do not realise that they have the power to be in charge, that their energy is everything, and that if they fix their energy they can fix their life! I am obsessed with helping people become aware of their energy, be intentional, live with awareness and agency, pay attention to what lifts and lowers them, and take action so that they can use their personal power to their advantage.

We live in a weird world! Our energy is scattered, and we are being pulled in so many directions. To be good at anything, we need to come back to ourselves – to what powers us, to what works for us. In the race to have and do and be everything, we have lost ourselves. We have lost the connection with where we get our energy. We need to understand our energy contributors and contaminators: who and what energises and drains us.

Energy comes from all levels. Physical energy comes from food, hydration and sleep, which nourish our bodies. Emotional energy arises from doing things that give us joy: laughter, fun and being with people we love. Mental energy is increased by becoming aware of the beliefs that weigh us down and shifting our heads into a more useful space. Connecting to our spiritual energy makes us feel safer and more trusting and allows us to build faith in ourselves.

Let's start at the beginning!

## We are all energetic beings

I believe that when you were born, your soul chose a body. Your soul moved in, literally! While there are many people bumping around on this planet thinking that they are humans having a spiritual experience, let me tell you that life changes when you flip that script. Believing that you are a soul having a physical experience is a game changer. You start to notice things. You start to see everything as information. You start collecting experiences and feelings and using them to improve the quality of your future experiences.

Living in a body is quite a ride. There is maintenance to do and a huge number of feelings to process. Relationships, arguments, grief, joy and heartache all take up space. They all deplete your energy. Think of your body like a bank statement of deposits and withdrawals: nothing goes unnoticed. Listening to your body, creating time and space to honour your mind and all of your energies, will change your life.

So, you are a soul riding around in a body, and your body needs fuel. The equation is pretty simple: what you put in you will get out. It's a case of cause and effect. Giving your body what it needs to be at its best is essential. You need to work with your body rather than against it.

The first 26 years of my life I did what I wanted. I arrogantly threw crap at my body and expected it to 'deal with it'. I worked on the assumption that my body worked for me, that it would take what I gave it. I had zero gratitude, and I was taking zero responsibility. And then my body spoke. It said, 'No more. This has to stop'. It held an intervention!

That took me on a two-year journey of re-establishing a relationship with my body. My body and I formed a partnership, like an arranged marriage. I committed to giving it what it needed, and it committed to keeping me moving, to allowing me to get on with living the big life I wanted to live.

This partnership required me to spend some time in my head, to unpack some of my beliefs and shift my mindset. I had to understand my mental energy.

Our energy starts with our thoughts. What we think has a massive impact on the reality we live in. Our emotions amplify our energy. We all have a feeling factory inside us, a building full of feelings and emotions. These all affect our energy. Feelings that get ignored or suppressed rot and create massive issues in our bodies. Our bodies hold onto everything. They store our thoughts, our unprocessed feelings and all the mental and emotional drama that we thought we had gotten away with!

This book is all about you and your energy: how you can get more of it, how you can guard your energy from the people who seem to be constantly on the take, and how you can build awareness around the ways that you give energy and understand what it's like to experience your energy.

Taking responsibility for my energy changed my life. I think it can change yours, too. Living well means we take the relevant actions to increase our energy and guard it from the people and places that drain us. It means taking charge of what our energy says about us and what we are putting out into the world, and how the world responds to us. It means avoiding what pulls us down and feasting on what lifts us up.

Are you ready to get aware, to take responsibility and to be intentional?

I am always complimented on my energy levels. I was once introduced at a conference as a 'human Berocca'! The greatest compliment I have ever received was from a man I did not know who walked up to me at an event and said, 'I love your vitality. You have life oozing out of you!'

People don't realise that my energy is something I spend a lot of time and effort on. More often than we want to admit, we are in control of the amount of energy that we have. Once we know what to do, we can contribute to building the energy that we need, and we can become aware of our contaminants – the things that take down our energy. They might be habits, humans or health issues. Some of them are very simple. Do you eat processed foods that weigh down your body and your immune system? Do you stay up late in front of a screen? Do you spend time with negative or angry people? Cause and effect: you eat or do something that drops your energy, and you feel the impact of that. Bad energy decisions result in bad energy!

Where do you get your energy from? You might get physical energy from a smoothie in the morning or a good night's sleep.

Your friends should be a source of positive emotional energy; if they are not, this is a big problem. At work, you also need to derive emotional energy from gorgeous people who make you happy, people who make it worth going to work – they literally make your day. The stuff that uplifts our minds and our hearts is our emotional energy and our mental energy. This is all the feel-good stuff that makes you super happy.

Then there's spiritual energy, which comes from feeling safe and connected. Being a soul driving around in a body means that you need to access your spiritual energy. Spiritual energy is about healing and protection. It's about connecting with your higher self, the essence of you. Spiritual energy is where you connect with your purpose, your worth and your intuition.

Having a belief system is like having energetic insurance: you have something to fall back on, something to lean into when you don't feel supported. When you have something bigger than yourself to plug into, you feel guided, assisted and supported.

People who have strong faith are uplifted and often have lots of energy. I get a lot of spiritual energy from my beliefs. I am not religious. I am a spiritual freelancer. I have my own beliefs, and they are carefully curated and tested over time. They are mine – not the beliefs I was 'given' as a child, nor the things that other people wanted me to believe. I have spent a huge amount of time examining and working out what beliefs work for me.

Connecting with your spiritual energy is not about wearing a kaftan and sandals. You do not have to wear flowers in your hair or 'become religious'. It is about connecting to your origin story, with who you were before the world told you who to be. It's about getting in touch with the essence of being *you* – what your energy says about you and how the world responds to what you are putting out!

## Your energy introduces you before you even speak

What does your energy say about you? We all are aware of energy to a point. Even if you do not consider yourself spiritual, intuitive or connected, you understand the experience of another person's energy. 'Their energy is a bit off', 'You could cut the air with a knife' and 'They didn't seem right' are all common sayings referring to someone's energy.

People send out energy through their body language. Smiles disarm us. We have all met people who gave us an immediate feeling of warmth. This lets you know that a positive flow of energy is taking place. We have also all met people who gave us an immediate feeling of weirdness and uncomfortableness! When you encounter someone who is angry, upset or uncomfortable within their own skin, they feel chaotic. We sometimes refer to negative or needy people as 'high-maintenance' as they tend to be a drain on your energy. Energy robbers take more than they give. Every human's energy has the ability to influence you, and yet so many people seem unaware of how they come across.

Once you are consciously aware of a person's energy, you get to make a decision: you get to be clever with your energy. You can choose to maximise positive energetic experiences such as love, support and enthusiasm, and you can minimise the stressful and painful energy caused by angry, negative, critical or needy people.

This book is about *all* of your energy! You are a combination of many energy sources:

- Your **physical energy** is the energy in your body, the simple decisions you make every hour that work for or against you. It's based on cause and effect and leads to a healthy you.

- Your **emotional energy** is the energy in your heart, how you contribute to or contaminate your world. It's based on feelings and emotions and leads to a happy you.
- Your **mental energy** is the energy in your head. It's based on mindset and belief and leads to an inspired you.
- Your **spiritual energy** is the energy in your soul that can support you. It's based on healing and protection and leads to a connected you.

Ultimately, understanding your energy is about creating the conditions for you to live in an amazing way, to get what you need so you can do what you want.

Your energy is your life force. It's the difference between you feeling amazing and not. Energy is a beast. When you have great energy, you are unstoppable. You are literally a force. When you don't have it, you are flat. You are tired and not physically or mentally at your best. You are unable to do the things that you want and need to do as you have no fuel in your tank, no pep in your step.

And when you are unaware of your energy, you push people away. The world responds to you, whether you are aware of it or not.

If there is one thing worth obsessing over, I think energy – *your* energy – is it. Get aware of it, get more of it and get intentional about how you use it, and you can feel and be strong and decide who and what deserves your magnificent life force.

## So, what is energy?

Energy is power, strength, force – the ability or capacity to produce an effect. The word energy comes from the Ancient Greek word 'energeia', coined by Aristotle, which means 'activity' or 'to be in action': the prefix 'en' means 'in', 'at', or 'within' and the root word 'ergon' means 'to function or work'.

I love the idea of energy meaning 'work within'. The word 'energetic' is defined as 'a capacity for intense activity'. There is no doubt that life is not for the meek, and modern-day life could definitely be described as an intense activity.

The opposite of energy would have to be fatigue. People often complain about the constant state of fatigue that they feel, the apathy as they struggle to get through their week. 'Burnout' is one of the most common words bounced around many workplaces.

One of our biggest challenges we face is that we want to have it all. We want to have incredible careers, perfect families, Instagram-worthy homes, beautiful bodies and holidays that make our friends green with envy. I believe in the power of want. I am very wanty. I am also realistic. I worked out very early in life that if I wanted a lot, I was going to need to have my shit together.

## When life takes you down

At the age of 26 I had an adrenal collapse. My body stopped working. I woke up one morning and could not get up; my head would not lift off the pillow. It was a crazily busy time in my life. I had just gotten married, project-managing a huge wedding where there was no detail not thought of! I was working long hours and travelling to the US regularly on work trips.

After five days of sweating and sleeping and barely being able to stand, I headed to the doctor. He told me that I probably had chronic fatigue, that it would take me years to recover and that I should plan to wind back my life to working three days a week.

I was not happy. I remember the feeling of powerlessness. I was furious at what the doctor had said. I had no interest in 'winding my life back': I did not want to be limited. As a full-on, high-energy overachiever, the idea of a long-term prognosis of laying around was not great.

I could barely stand up to shower, and I remember my mum dressing me like I was a toddler. After several weeks of sleeping, I went to see a friend of my mother's for a massage. Pat was more than a masseuse: she was a Touch for Health practitioner. Trained in muscle testing and kinesiology, Pat said that I needed an overhaul and suggested that I go to a naturopath.

I did not know where to start, so I did what we all did back in 1996 and 'let my fingers do the walking': I flicked through the Yellow Pages and found a naturopath. Michael was a naturopath and osteopath, and he looked more like a builder than a natural healer! The irony was, he rebuilt me! Calmly and kindly, he reset my body and retaught me everything that I knew up to that point. I remember him teaching me how to walk! Slowly, consciously, feeling my feet, my hips leading the way while I concentrated on my breathing. It was a stark contrast to my forward-leaning rushing around, short steps and even shorter breaths as I dashed from place to place.

I realised that I had been abusing my body. I was demanding and expecting it to function without giving a thought to what my body needed from me. I had blocked out all the signals, chugging down Panadol and coffee every time my body signalled that I had any pain, tension or waning energy. I was flogging my body.

I was living on bread and cheese and coffee. Michael asked me what two foods I would fight him for. I told him I would never give up bread and cheese. He looked me deep in my eyes and said, 'That's what we are going to do'.

Over the next six months, I fasted. I became a pescatarian. I took loads of supplements and read everything I could get my hands on.

Michael said I had to make some choices. I could continue to treat my body like a hotel, or I could make it a home. I could continue carelessly eating and drinking and ignoring my body's concerns, or I could 'live big'. He told me that I would get out what I put in, that living an energetic and full life was a decision. I was sold. Living big had always been what I wanted. Stupidly, I had not connected the law of cause and effect! It hadn't occurred to me that I was getting out of my body what I was putting in!

Pat gave me a copy of Louise Hay's book *You Can Heal Your Life*. I realised that I wasn't respecting my body because I didn't like it. I was miles away from self-love. I was suffering from bad case of NGE – 'not good enough' – and somehow thought that I could make myself a high performer by not caring for myself.

Michael taught me about nutrition, he taught me about breathing and supplements, but most of all he taught me about respect. He taught me about how clever and extraordinary our bodies are and how wonderful they can be when we join forces with our bodies rather than working against them.

I am forever grateful to Pat, Michael and Louise Hay for what I learnt from them. I learnt that I was only going to get out of my body what I put into it, that I was creating everything that was happening in my body and my life, and that I had the power to be the difference I wanted.

From that moment on, every decision I made was in collaboration with my body. I listened. I checked in. I became incredibly aware of how my body responded to food, to toxins, to different temperatures. My body and mind became partners. I understood physical and mental energy. Spiritual energy was next. Pat lent me books and taught me about auras. She used a small slide projector to fill her tiny room with colour so I could lie and absorb the vibrancy of whatever colour I needed at the time. She taught me that humans are absorbent, and that colour and energy could be felt and absorbed.

What I thought was the worst thing that had ever happened to me quickly became the best.

## Embracing the power of energy

Energy is the essence of our existence. In this book, I invite you to embark on a journey of self-discovery and empowerment through the lens of energy. Each chapter includes tips and quick wins to impact your energy instantly.

Ultimately, this journey is about creating the conditions for you to live your best life. Your energy is your life force. When it's abundant, you're unstoppable; when it wanes, you're limited. By gaining awareness, taking responsibility and being intentional about your energy, you can transform your life. Are you ready to become conscious, aware and intentional about your energy? Are you prepared to embrace the power within you?

Everything is energy, and that is all there is to it. It's your responsibility to shield yourself from energy drainers and embrace what uplifts you. Your energy is your superpower, and it's time to harness it for a life that's truly magnificent.

# 2

# PHYSICAL ENERGY

*'Rhythm is our universal mother tongue.*
*It's the language of the soul.'*
~ Gabrielle Roth

You deserve to feel good! Feeling good is your birthright. It is also your responsibility. It is your job to give your body what it needs to feel good.

When my physical energy is good, I feel strong and supple and hydrated. I sleep well. My health is good. My body feels good. As we age, maintaining our physical energy can become harder. I write 'can' because I do not believe that it has to. I think it takes a bit more effort and care, but age doesn't have to mean that our physical energy is diminished. I have found that the older I get, the more considerate I need to be to my body. I need to take more care be more care-full.

## Caring for ourselves

When I wrote my book *Juggling in High Heels* and used the word 'care-full', my editor kept coming back to me saying it was spelt incorrectly. I explained that I did not mean 'careful' as in avoiding danger and harm but 'care-full' – full of care.

I am very care-full with my body. I am care-full to get enough sleep, take my supplements and fill my meals with nutritious ingredients. My body used to be able to stay up late, wolf down processed foods and knock back several wines with no impact. Now, if I do those things, I feel it. I feel heavy and achy and a bit wrecked.

I often meet people who complain about ageing. They whinge as if their body is against them. They are ungrateful and unkind to their bodies. Their bodies are doing their best with very little kindness or consideration in return. You don't have to be a sluggish, overweight, achy mess. You need to get aware and start making decisions that support your body rather than compromising it.

I believe if you take care of your body, it will take care of you. Honour your body with the respect it deserves. I have always thought of my body as a rental car that I collected at birth and will return when I die. It's the only one I'm going to get, and it cannot be traded in! In the space in between birth and death, it is my responsibility to run it well – give it good fuel, hydrate it daily and be proactive around maintenance and medical needs. Your body is a vehicle for your soul to drive around in! As American entrepreneur Jim Rohn said, 'Take care of your body. It's the only place you have to live'.

Often in busy periods of our lives we do not have the time or resources to look after ourselves. So, we need to find ways of honouring our bodies in microdoses. I call these 'pockets of perfect'. How can you add a tiny pocket of perfect into your day? It might be lying in the back seat of your car; it might be walking on grass with bare feet; it might be sitting at the beach. Pockets of perfect are small, intentional breaks that honour your body and increase your energy.

When your body feels good, you have more energy. It's a pretty simple equation. There are lots of things that you can 'do' for increased physical energy, but there are also lots of tools you can buy to support your body. The obvious things are a good bed, a decent office chair for work and supportive walking shoes. Having a body requires investment. Spending money on tools, training and treats all support your energy. Treats might include a textured shakti acupressure mat under your desk at work, a massage gun beside the couch for de-stressing tired muscles at the end of each day, a foam roller for rolling out your back or legs while watching TV, a firm bolster pillow for under your legs when lying on the couch or an aromatherapy diffuser next to your bed.

Think of your body as your friend. Give it what it needs to function well and you will benefit!

Noticing what your body needs takes some effort. You need to connect to how your body is feeling. Take time to check in, to listen to the messages and wisdom that your body is holding. Taking time to move out of your head and connect with your body is the first step. You cannot love something you do not feel connected to. You need to make time to connect and be in awe of your incredible body.

Awe means 'reverential respect, mixed with wonder'. I am in constant awe of what our bodies can do and *do* do! Our hearts beat, our joints bend and our eyes see. Take a moment to consider the crazy systems that are living and working in your body right now!

I do this with a vertical check-in:

1. Lie down.
2. Breathe slowly for a few breaths.
3. Wiggle your finger and your toes. Roll your limbs from side to side.
4. How are your feet feeling? Are they sore or tired?
5. How do your legs feel? Are they heavy or restless?
6. How do your hips and bum feel? Are they tight and clenched?
7. How is your tummy? Is it uneasy or knotty?
8. How does your chest feel? Is it tight or restricted?
9. How do your shoulders feel? Are the heavy and burdened?
10. How is your head? Is it foggy or tense?

Having regular check-ins with your body is important. Listen to it. Ask it questions. Your body holds so much wisdom and is constantly sending you signals; it will show you what you need if you listen carefully. Our bodies manifest our emotions.

Louise Hay's book *You Can Heal Your Life* taught me so much about this. Over 50 million copies of this book have been sold; it is a game changer in drawing the connection between ailments and affirmations, showing the connection between our thoughts and how they manifest in our bodies. *You Can Heal Your Life*, Inna Segal's book *The Secret Language of Your Body* and Annette Noontil's *The Body is the Barometer of the Soul* are all excellent books on the connection between your body and your thoughts and emotions.

## Becoming friends with our bodies

There are three types of people:

1. **There are people who misuse their bodies.** They have no respect for how incredibly lucky they are to have a fully functioning body. This misuse shows up in an extreme lack of care, often bordering on self-abuse. It shows up in not sleeping, drinking chemical 'energy' drinks, eating heavily processed foods and using drugs and alcohol.
2. **There are people who use their bodies.** They act like they own their bodies. They think their bodies are infinite sources of energy that they can do whatever they like with. They take what they can without any regard for what their bodies need. Many of us do this when we are young! We act like we are unstoppable. Continuing this misuse as we age is very damaging and destructive.
3. **There are people who are in partnership with their bodies.** When we become friends with our bodies, we join them in partnership, like a deal: I'll be good to you if you are good to me! We are in touch with what our bodies need and want, and we spend time and money looking after our bodies.

Our relationships with our bodies are often difficult. When we are young, we often think that we are bulletproof. We think that our bodies will do what we want. We choose to do terrible things to our bodies in exchange for being thin, or fun, or a good time at a party. As we age, we become more aware. We notice how much we need sleep, how our body doesn't process alcohol as well as it used to, that not moving causes it to seize up.

Unfortunately, some people realise this too late. They have already messed up their bodies in ways that they may not be able to heal from.

Making peace with your body is about acceptance. It is about being grateful. You may not be as tall or as slim as you like. You might think that you got a rough deal when bodies were being handed out! However, try thinking about your body and all the wonderful things it has done for you. I am grateful that my knees can bend down to pick things up off the floor, that my arms can carry my groceries home, that my neck can turn to show me what's behind me, that my body moves and beats and transports blood in my veins.

We spend way too much time being critical, comparing our bodies to others' and wishing that our bodies were different. Our heads judge our bodies. They obsess over the ideal way we 'should' look instead of being able to simply honour and enjoy how we *do* look. When we step into awe, we allow ourselves to see how magnificent our bodies are. Our arms, while they may not be as slim as we might like, allow us to hug our loved ones. Our legs, while they might be dimpled and dented, take us to the most magical places!

We are all different. Being born to a tiny mother really helped me with my body image. I was bigger than my mother when

I was 11. My first bra was bigger than hers is now! I realised that there was nothing to do but accept the body I had. I was constantly compared to my mum, with people commenting about how tiny she was (and quietly judging that I was not!).

Someone once told me that dogs don't compare themselves to other dogs. Corgis don't go around wishing they were greyhounds; they just get on with being the best corgis that they can be. My mum was a chihuahua; I was a labrador. There was nothing that could be done.

This is what led me into my career as a stylist. I wanted to show people that they could look great. Regardless of size or weight or height, I believe that everyone can look amazing. There are tricks for lengthening short bodies and slimming down thicker areas, but most people who look amazing look that way because they feel amazing. They like themselves and have packaged themselves accordingly. They see clothing as a celebration and expression of themselves, not as a tarpaulin required to cover themselves up!

Making friends with your body gives you a companion, a partner in life. Imagine having a friend who was there for you 24 hours a day, who took you everywhere, who lifted everything for you, who sucked in air and filtered it for you, who transported oxygen around your blood cells, who grew new fingernails, who replaced your skin cells and who healed your cuts and bruises. What a wonderful friend that would be! Wouldn't you want to honour that friend by providing them with the most gorgeous and comfortable space for them to sleep in, the most nourishing food, the purest water and fabric they love to wrap themselves in?

Making friends with your body can lead to one of the most amazing relationships of your life. You are partners, till death do you part!

I love this poem by Hollie Holden:

*Today I asked my body what she needed,*
*Which is a big deal*
*Considering my journey of*
*Not Really Asking That Much.*

*I thought she might need more water.*
*Or protein.*
*Or greens.*
*Or yoga.*
*Or supplements.*
*Or movement.*

*But as I stood in the shower*
*Reflecting on her stretch marks,*
*Her roundness where I would like flatness,*
*Her softness where I would like firmness,*
*All those conditioned wishes*
*That form a bundle of*
*Never-Quite-Right-Ness,*
*She whispered very gently:*

*Could you just love me like this?*

~ Hollie Holden, June 2016

When you are friends with your body, you become more caring. You become more interested in your body's preferences. What foods does your body prefer, what fabrics, what temperatures?

As your awareness increases, you become aware of what you are putting in your body. You start noticing your cravings. When I am stressed, I crave crunchy things. When I am angry, I want spicy things. When I am feeling sorry for myself, I want sugar. Our feelings show up in our diets. We end up in a shit cycle of feeling like shit, eating like shit and then behaving like shit (see figure 1)!

Figure 1: the cycle of shit

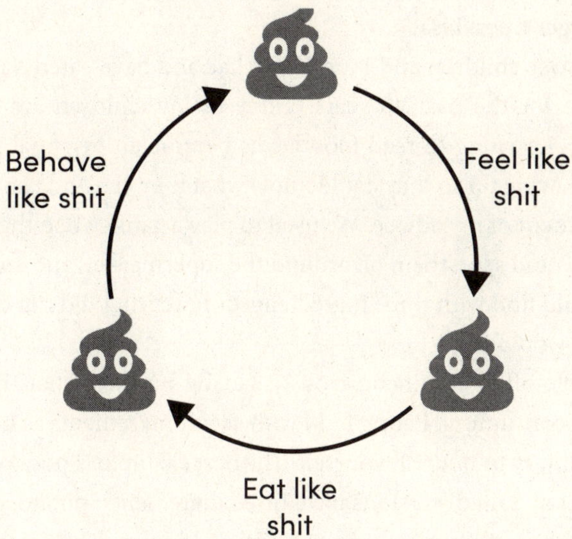


## Nourish your body

There are many ways we can nourish our bodies. Providing nourishment means providing the substances necessary for good health, growth and condition.

Food fuels our bodies. Food is needed for our internal functions and repairs, to build and maintain our cells and body tissues. The combination of nutrients and hydration is required for our bodies to be active and interact with the physical world. As Hippocrates said way back in the fifth century BC, 'Let food be thy medicine and medicine be thy food.'

I remember the moment that my naturopath, Michael, told me I was only to eat wholefoods. He told me that before I put anything into my mouth I needed to check if it was something that had grown whole. As I walked out the door he said, 'There are no hamburger trees, Lisa!'

My four children and I are all coeliac and have eaten a gluten-free diet for the past 20 years. Three of my children are type 1 diabetic. Learning to read food labels became an essential part of them growing up so they could know what they can and cannot eat independent of my advice. We used to play a game when they were little: I would send them off around the supermarket, and anything they could find with three ingredients or fewer that did not contain gluten I would buy.

People often eat unconsciously, having no idea what they are actually consuming. Eating food with as few ingredients as possible is a great way to nourish yourself. The best example is potato chips. Most 'ready salted' versions have three ingredients: potato, oil and salt. Flavoured varieties have as many as 18 ingredients – they are loaded up with powders, flavourings, food acids and enhancers. There are many foods sold today that I think should be labelled 'contains food-like substances'.

Before my kids were diagnosed, I had never read a food label, I had never dieted or calorie counted, but reading food labels blew my mind. Now, I am obsessed with the quality of the ingredients that I put into my body. I want a quality life. I want to have amazing energy, and I want to assist my body rather than working against it.

I have never been concerned with weight loss. Because my mother is so small, I never had the experience growing up of living with someone who 'watched their weight'. I was never introduced to diet culture. I remember going to a friend's house and opening her fridge, and it was full of stuff I had never seen before, like low-fat salad dressing, skim milk and processed products designed for people concerned with weight loss.

There is a huge difference between eating for health and eating for thin. Thin is the goal for so many people. They neglect crucial nutrients and sabotage their organs in an effort to be a smaller pants size. Eating for health is about giving your body what it needs to get the best out of it – the best now in the energy you are able to expend and the best for longevity, to keep your body functioning well for as long as possible!

It amazes me that people so often put their bodies last when making food decisions. It's simple: if you eat rubbish, you will feel like rubbish.

Another issue is that loads of people have intolerances and are unaware of them! Many experts suggest that high stress and the consumption of large amounts of processed foods are leading people's immune systems to become more and more intolerant to different foods.

Symptoms of gluten intolerance, for example, can be as apparent as bloating and farting or as seemingly unrelated as mouth ulcers and reflux. Many children these days are eating gluten eight or more times a day. Breakfast cereals, toast, muesli bars, muffins, sandwiches, instant noodles, flavoured potato chips and biscuits all contain gluten. It can also be found in processed meats like ham and bacon, as well as packaged stocks, sauces and salad dressings. Throw in a dinner made from a packet and that adds up to a lot of gluten. Put simply, my body doesn't like it, and I know I'm not the only one. People who burp and fart a lot, have sore and swollen tummies, are tired and grumpy and experience rashes, aches and pains should investigate whether they have a food intolerance.

I haven't eaten gluten or lactose for years and this has hugely improved my energy levels. Some friends comment on how hard it must be to follow a strict gluten-free diet, but I don't find it hard at all. Coeliac disease has been a gift to our family. We are now healthy, energetic and happy. We bake a lot and love to eat pies, cakes and pancakes; we simply use ingredients that don't contain gluten.

It's worth finding out exactly what is in your food. Not everyone has food allergies, but many of us have food intolerances. These can be hard to diagnose, and in my experience the medical profession can be reluctant to help. So many people have told me they have been tested and they don't have food intolerances. Coeliac tests often come back negative because there is not enough gluten in the body to pass a test, which makes sense because people who are intolerant of a particular food often naturally stay away from it as it causes their bodies discomfort.

This is most obvious in small children. If you have a small child that consistently resists a particular food, don't force it on them – you will be overriding their in-built guidance system. A friend's daughter would not eat potatoes, not even fries at a party. A year later, she found she was allergic to potatoes! The child had instinctively known the whole time!

Keeping a food diary for a week – not to measure food intake but to track your body's responses – is a smart thing to do. This is not a judgement diary; it's a record of your energy, so you can work out when you're feeling great and when you're not. Write down how you feel every hour – tired, heavy, gassy – and write down everything you eat. What you ate two hours before will contribute to how you are feeling. Tracking the foods that give you great energy, that work well with your body, that your body appreciates, is a very smart exercise.

Whole and pure foods are some of my greatest pleasures. Strolling a market and buying directly from a grower or artisan producer fills me with joy! I love buying organic ingredients. Apart from the amazing flavours and quality of ingredients grown well without chemical intervention, I get the most amazing feeling. I feel responsible, I feel honourable and I feel conscious. Each ingredient is consciously chosen, and I can feel my body delight in my choices. Buying organic means the food was produced without synthetic pesticides and herbicides. Supporting organic shops and suppliers means you are contributing to the shift away from conventional industrial agriculture. Our current food system relies heavily on toxic chemicals for crop cultivation. By supporting organically grown food, you are not only feeding your soul, you are also supporting food producers who don't make their workers come into contact with pesticides. Eating organic is a win for you, animals, workers and the environment.

You are what you eat, so do not be easy, cheap, fast or fake! Here are some energy food tips:

- **Make friends with fat.** Stop avoiding healthy fats. The oils found in olives, avocados, coconuts and nuts are so good for us. Good fats help give us energy, protect our organs, support cell growth, keep cholesterol and blood pressure under control, and help your body absorb vital nutrients.
- **Eat protein at every meal.** There is no need to eat a Fred Flintstone–sized steak, but a portion of protein the size of your palm is perfect. Using your palm as a guide is way easier than weighing and measuring food; one-size-fits-all is no good because we all have different-sized bodies!

- **Enjoy your food.** Food consumed with guilt will be noticed by your body. Your body will contract and make it harder to process. While it's important for your overall health to eat wholefoods as much as possible, if you are going to sit down to a piece of cake, relax and enjoy it!
- **Learn about food.** Every single one of us has food in our lives every single day. Learn about where food comes from. Take an interest in what you are putting into your mouth.
- **Get good at cooking.** Start small. Learn one or two dishes. The average human eats around 90,000 meals in a lifetime! If you eat, it makes sense to be able to cook. I have spent the past year teaching my youngest son how to cook. He said, 'Why are you so keen on cooking?' I replied, 'Because I love to eat!'
- **Buy food that is as fresh as possible and grown as close to your door as possible.** The closer to source your food is, the higher its level of nutrients. Don't buy vegetables imported from another country that have been sitting in a shipping container for months! Eat seasonal food and buy locally.

I am not puritan. I love cakes and fried food and treats, and I regularly enjoy foods that I love, but my north star for any meal prep or food selection is body first. What does my body need? If I have had a week of eating out, enjoying divine restaurants and sipping champagne, then I know that my body needs simplicity. It needs veggies and water and enzyme support to give it a helping hand. I see my body as a partner: I love my body and I want to help her, to nourish her and to notice her.

Your food, hydration and nutrients are so bloody important. I work on the theory that your food should power you for three hours. That means it needs to be fit for purpose, as whatever you're eating and drinking will significantly impact your energy. For example, if I'm presenting at a big conference, I have to make sure to have plenty of protein and water before I go on stage. Otherwise, I get tired and dehydrated, and my brain stops working – which is not a good thing! If I eat too many carbohydrates, I feel fantastic to start with thanks to that tremendous boost carbs give you for the first ten minutes, but then I really struggle to keep my energy going.

If you feel wrecked in the afternoon, you might reach for a sugary hit, but chances are you will crash again soon after. Think about what you're eating and the result it has on your energy. Often at night we sit, eat, watch TV, then possibly eat some more. But unless you've got a wild sex life or some other exciting activity planned for 10 p.m., you don't need to be eating all night. Eat for your energy needs.

I am not good on limitations – I am greedy by nature. I am grateful that my body reacts badly to gluten and dairy as that eliminates lots of things I would probably want to eat! When you eat good ingredients, you do not have to limit yourself. No one ever said 'you are only allowed one cauliflower'!

## Water

Water is your body's most important nutrient. It helps facilitate the chemical reactions that produce energy from food. All of our bodily functions need water to work. Water lubricates our eyes, noses, muscles and mouth. It cleans our body, producing urine, waste and perspiration. It protects our soft tissues and regulates our temperature. And yet so many people treat drinking water like an optional activity! Staying hydrated helps your body to do its thing. Dehydrated bodies have less energy because the body has to work harder to make the basic processes happen.

Up to 60% of the human adult body is water. The brain and heart are composed of around 70% water, and the lungs are around 80% water. Keeping these important pieces of our human machinery topped up is essential.

My best hydration strategy is to drink one glass of water every hour I am awake. In a perfect day that is 16 glasses of water, or 4 litres. Given that nothing is ever perfect, even I miss four to six glasses I am still getting 2.5 to 3.5 litres a day. I also have a rule that if someone offers me a drink, I have water. I don't turn down water. It keeps me ahead of my water intake.

## Supplement support

Nurturing is the act of caring for and protecting something. Supplements are a wonderful way of nurturing your body. For example, we can use fish oils to care for our joints.

There are loads of opinions on supplements. Do we need them? Should we take them? My opinion is yes! Here is my logic: Even if we ate the perfect diet every single day of our lives, we cannot meet some of the basic vitamin and mineral requirements for excellent health as in many places our soil is depleted of the minerals that are needed to grow food well. And I have never met anyone who eats the perfect diet! I like to use supplements to balance out my body's bank account. I am able to add and alter the levels of vitamins and minerals that I need depending on what my body needs.

I do this in partnership with a naturopath. I am not qualified to know all of the things that my body needs, and I think good advice is essential. While swallowing a multivitamin might give you some backup, without the right help it is hard to know if the ratios of ingredients are effective for you or the next person. There are simple equations a naturopath will know that can very quickly change your energy levels.

If you have trouble getting out of bed in the morning, you could be low in potassium. And if you have trouble sleeping at night, you could be low in magnesium. These are simple things that are easy to correct, and lots of us are quite deficient in them.

I have been working with a naturopath for the past 30 years. A naturopath will consider your lifestyle, diet and any illnesses, offering support while considering all the systems in your body. Regular osteopath or chiropractor visits keep your spine and joints in alignment and increase blood flow to muscles and tissue. Regular massage relieves muscle tension, reduces stress hormones and increases joint mobility. Having a proactive health support team of an osteopath, a massage therapist and a naturopath means I very rarely get sick. I believe that prevention is better than cure.

I also believe that my body deserves support. Some people spend more time and money on getting their cars serviced than they spend on their bodies! If you want high-performance health, you need a pit crew!

## Nourishing yourself with colour

I love colour. I love food. I love colourful food! Food is energy and colour is energy. Brightly coloured foods are loaded with vitamins and antioxidants. Not only do we need more colour in our wardrobes, but we also need it in our fridges and our bodies.

If you have two foods to choose from, always go with the one with the most natural colour. Natural, brightly coloured foods almost always have high amounts of vitamins and nutrients. I am not talking about cupcakes here, although I do believe that bright, colourful French macaroons are so good for your soul that your body will not mind one bit!

When my children were little, we played a game to see who had eaten the most colour during the day. My kids loved this game. Roasting beetroot, nibbling on blueberries and drinking carrot juice are all things that can increase your colour intake. We would list off the number of colours each of us had eaten that day at dinner. This game made me more creative with meals. I would buy yellow capsicums, blueberries, grapes, eggplant, yams – anything I could find that had interesting colours. We talk all the time about eating our greens, but what about our blues, reds, purples and yellows?

Try to fit in ten brightly coloured foods per day. I aim for three to five green foods, three red or purple foods and two orange foods. Check in with the rest of your household at dinner time to see how many colours you have each eaten during the day. Spinach, carrots, capsicum, brown rice and pink salmon look so much better on a plate than white rice covered in mince. It is also much better for you.

Imagine if everything you ate was fresh, whole, colourful and chemical-free! Maybe this is not achievable every day, but if more days are like that then you are winning. It's cheaper, tastier and better for you than crap from packets.

We all have times when we are busy or travelling and we don't have access to the foods we want to eat. Travelling and attending events, I can have weeks of awful buffets, lunch on the run and late hotel meals. My fix for this is broth.

My naturopath Michael put me onto potassium broth 25 years ago when my body was in crisis. I still make it often.

### Potassium broth

Get a large pot and roughly chop:

- 2 potatoes
- 2 large carrots
- 4 beetroot tops with leaves on
- 6 leaves of silverbeet or kale
- 4 sticks of celery with leaves on
- 2 handfuls of parsley
- 2 cloves of garlic
- 6 peppercorns.

All veggies should be organic, or at least spray-free and unpeeled. Cover with water and bring to the boil. Simmer for one hour, then strain and discard the vegetables. Heat and drink when required.

I often make this after a big week. It gives my body nutrients and colour and goodness without asking her to process any food or do any work. It's like giving her the weekend off! There are many broths available that you can buy if you don't want to make your own.

I think of my body as a bank balance. There are times when I make massive withdrawals: I eat badly, I don't sleep enough and I push my body hard. Then, there are times when I curl up in blankets and drink broth and give her all the love and support I can, making deposits so I don't get overdrawn!

## Nourishing yourself with rest

As a high-energy overachiever, I've never been very good at rest.

Ten years ago, I could feel my body struggling. I knew it needed something. Ironically, what it needed was nothing – to do nothing!

I signed up for a retreat. At this retreat I met Neal. Neal is a contemporary yoga teacher who is obsessed with rest and kindness – kindness in every sense, but he became my teacher of self-kindness. I started doing restorative yoga. Restorative yoga is completely different than achievement yoga. I did not have to be flexible; I did not have to twist my body into weird shapes. I just needed to lie down!

We all gathered blankets and bolsters and cushions and were taught how to set up different poses. Each pose created a supported space for me to lie – on my back, on my side, sometimes even face-down. As I lay crumpled on the floor, pretending I was comfortable and trying to be low-maintenance, Neal wandered over. He could tell I was not comfortable. He could see that my joints were unsupported! He quietly moved about rolling blankets and moving pillows until I was completely blissed out!

He then asked me the most amazing question: 'Is there any way you could be more comfortable right now?' I was practically dribbling at this point. I had never felt so safe or cared for in my life! A lightweight piece of muslin was draped over my eyes, and I am pretty sure I fell asleep.

We did two more of these 'set ups' that day – one after a yummy lunch and the third after dinner. Neal then announced that lights out would be 9 p.m.! I had been 'sleeping' all day. *No chance of me sleeping tonight*, I thought.

How wrong I was! I was sound asleep at 9.05 p.m. and slept blissfully. It turns out the more you sleep, the more you sleep!

That weekend changed my life. I became more aware of my body; I became very mindful of how I moved and what my body needed. There was a delightful deliberateness that was a huge contrast from my rushing and chaotic life.

I remember the last morning, everyone sat around in a large circle. The faces were softer and their eyes were glossy. Neal reminded us all that this should be our normal state! I left there with the message loud and clear that rest was my friend. My head felt clear and my body was calm. I have been doing these retreats two or three times each year ever since. It took me until I was 40 to realise that high-performance people need high-performance rest!

I also have a 'rest nest' permanently set up at home. Blankets, bolsters and cushions are laid out in a Lisa shape, ready for me to flop into at any time. Because of the amount of support offered by a restorative pose, you rest even more deeply than sleep. One hour in my nest and I feel like I have had a whole night's sleep! I often drag all the pillows and blankets off the beds in hotel rooms to create a resting space.

Shortly after I met Neal, I met Karla Brodie. Karla is a teaching colleague of Neal's and an incredible teacher of rest and contemporary yoga. Karla has taught me about surrender, and allowing, and being curious with what my body needs while in rest. I have this gorgeous piece from her journal *An Invitation to Rest* on my wall to remind me to rest often!

*Find a way to the earth.*
*Rest there. Surrender any*
*effort or thought or knowing*
*or unknowing.*

*Everything right now*
*Could be considered on a*
*Spectrum of deep meaning*
*And knowing to no meaning*
*and not knowing.*

*Be as you are – the*
*brilliance of just that,*
*You and the wonder of*
*your trillions of cells, the*
*extraordinary-ness of you*
*As you are; skin, heart*
*Bones, blood, breath…*

~ Karla Brodie

## The importance of sleep

The most significant source of energy available to us is sleep. The quality and quantity of your sleep has an enormous impact on your energy. We intellectually know this, but it blows my mind how many people do not prioritise sleep!

The right amount of sleep is critical to your performance. An adult between the ages of 19 and 55 needs eight hours of sleep every day. You'll die from sleep deprivation before food deprivation: it takes two weeks to starve, but ten days without sleep can kill you.

So many adults think that good sleep is optional rather than essential. Sleep is a basic need for all humans to be at their best. While you are sleeping, your brain recharges. Your cells repair themselves. Your body releases important hormones. Just because we are able to operate on a small amount of sleep doesn't not mean that we should. Sleep is not a luxury. Exhaustion is not cool. Turning up to work well rested and ready to give your best for the next eight hours is cool!

Often, it is not our fault that we are terrible at sleeping. Sleep apnoea, menopause, pregnancy and young children will all interfere with our ability to sleep. There will be many reasons throughout our lives why sleep just doesn't seem to work, but it is so powerful when we get it right. Sleep is about both quality and quantity. What are you doing to make sure you're getting the most amount of sleep possible?

The amount of sleep you are getting is often about when you choose to go to bed. Choosing your own bedtime is one of the few benefits of being an adult. As a child, it was all you wanted to do – you were desperate to be able to choose when you went to bed. Now that you are an adult, you have given away your power! You have fucked up your privilege! Being tired is dumb. Putting yourself to bed at a time that supports future you, the you that has to be awesome tomorrow, is smart. When people complain about being tired, I always translate that as them admitting that they're not very clever! People complain about being tired as if it is a badge of honour, but I think turning up to work tired is unprofessional and arrogant. Wandering around all day telling people you are tired is admitting that you are not clever enough to put yourself to bed at a reasonable time!

You might think that you can't sleep. For most people, this is a belief – it's a mindset, not a fact. Some say they can't sleep before midnight. This is your head sabotaging you. Listen to your talk about sleep – you will learn a lot about what stories your head is making up! You *can* sleep before midnight, but you may have to go to bed four hours earlier!

Getting in charge of your bedtime is very important. I set the alarm on my phone to go to bed. When it goes off, I know I've got to go. That sounds strange, but as a busy woman, I forget to go to bed. Having an alarm to remind me to that I need to make clever choices helps enormously. My intention to go to bed on time can easily be overridden when I get busy doing something and hours vanish before my eyes!

## Sleep quality

The second most important aspect of sleep after length is quality. If you're tossing and turning and not sleeping well, there are a whole lot of things you can do. Taking magnesium can help. I use magnesium oil on my legs every night as well as taking magnesium supplements. The temperature of your room is very important. So is controlling light – making your room as dark as possible will help your body to rest better.

There are lots of things you can try if sleep is challenging. Making sure you have an excellent environment for sleeping is important. Do you need a new bed? Old mattresses or uneven springs can make a night very unrestful. Once you have the bed sorted, what type of sheets do you like? Smooth and slippery? Rough linen? High-thread-count cotton? There's nothing better than getting into a bed made with gorgeous sheets! What you wear also makes a difference: fluffy PJs, tiny wee shorts or nothing at all?

One tip my gorgeous friend the late, great Kerry Henderson shared with me was mouth taping. Kerry was ahead of his time in many respects and learnt loads of yoga breathing techniques in the 1980s. He slept every night with his mouth taped. Mouth taping forces you to breathe through your nose when you sleep. When you breathe through your nose, your sinuses naturally produce nitric oxide. Nitric oxide has been proven to lower blood pressure and increase circulation. Breathing through the nose is relaxing – which is why it is often recommended along with yoga and meditation – so it makes sense as a way to create good sleep.

I find that when I tape my mouth, I sleep deeper and longer. It's incredibly relaxing. You only need a small piece of tape in the centre of your lips, not a full-blown mouth-covering gag! I strongly suggest giving it a shot. Practise by watching TV with your mouth taped.

One of the best books I've ever read about sleep is *The Sleep Revolution* by Arianna Huffington. She's an incredible woman. She collapsed one day in her office at *The Huffington Post*, smashed her head open and ended up in the hospital. She wasn't unwell or sick, just tired. She collapsed from pure exhaustion.

Arianna talks about changing your life one night at a time. When you sleep, everything changes. Your body heals, your mind rests and you grow. So many beautiful things happen when you're sleeping. You get to dream, and your soul travels the Earth. Huge problems can arise if you're not getting enough sleep. One of my favourite parts from the book is where Ariana writes about 'sleeping your way to the top'. People who sleep well literally have more chance of success.

## Creating a 'closing ceremony'

Part of making sleep a priority is creating a 'closing ceremony'. When I worked in retail, we had a routine at the end of the day to close the shop. Closing down at the end of the day means that you finish things properly. I always suggest that anyone who wants to improve their sleep creates a closing ceremony.

Start an hour before your decided bedtime. Drink a relaxing tea – something that signals to your body it's nearly time! I love lots of different combinations of chamomile, lavender, valerian root and passionflower. At this point, it's a good idea to say goodbye to technology and bright lights.

I like to stretch, roll onto my back and massage my feet with magnesium cream to relax and nourish my feet. I do an end-of-day skincare routine, sometimes including a bath or shower, and I then read or listen to a guided meditation for 20 minutes.

Epsom salt baths are excellent if you have had a big day. Epsom salt is magnesium sulphate and is sold in bags at most supermarkets. The magnesium helps restore electrolyte balance, muscle and nerve function, soothing muscle soreness and discomfort. If you don't have access to a bath, a foot bath will also feel amazing. I have ended many large days running events by soaking my feet in a hotel-room sink.

Be patient when you change your bedtime, as it takes a couple of weeks for your body to adapt to a new habit.

As well as a closing ceremony, I like to have an opening ceremony for the morning. Starting your day with gratitude and breathing is a way better start than sleeping through your alarm and dashing out of bed swearing!

## Exercise

Movement is essential. We are designed to move. The best kind of movement is the kind that feels good. Whether you enjoy lifting weights, rolling on the floor or long-distance running, I wish more people moved in a way they wanted to rather than how they 'should'. You 'should' do whatever feels good – as long as you are moving.

The benefits of exercise are proven and incontestable. Even as little as ten minutes of vigorous exercise a day can add years to your life. To allow disease to take root by being sedentary does not honour the sacred vessel that is your body.

Exercise almost guarantees that you will sleep better! It gives your cells more energy and circulates oxygen. Exercising can lead to higher brain dopamine levels, which helps elevate mood.

Four years ago, I had laser surgery on some veins in my legs. One of the post-op rules was that I had to walk for 45 minutes every day for four weeks. I started off well! Then life happened. I missed the odd day, then I was only walking on the odd day! I didn't think it mattered a huge amount as I am on my feet all day and pretty active. When I went for my final check, my surgeon asked me about my walking, and I told a wee fib and said, 'Oh yes, been doing that!' He examined my legs and said, 'You haven't been doing the walking!' I laughed and asked him how he knew. He said that he had put some dye into my veins, and if I had been doing the required walking it would have been gone. My dye was still there!

I told him that I was busy and active and moved a lot. He told me that walking nonstop for 45 minutes was essential for good cardiovascular health, for the workings of my veins, blood vessels and heart. I had never thought about the impact of exercise on my internal organs. I always thought about daily exercise as being good for weight and fitness – I knew it was good for the outcome of my arse – but thinking about it as something that kept my organs working was a game changer for me.

Caroline Williams' book *Move: The new science of body over mind* is excellent; I wish it had been written 20 years earlier as it completely changed my thinking about exercise. I learnt that lifting weights can boost your memory, working your core can reduce stress and walking stimulates your creativity!

For years I considered exercise a punishment. Now I see it as a celebration!

I was never a fan of cardio. I watch people out running and it looks like punishment! They tell me that they enjoy it and I believe some of them; some people love the feeling of cardio, and I love that for them. However, I know many people who work out because they hate their body. They work out because of fear: fear that they will get fat; fear that they will get old. Shifting from fear to love is something I am constantly attuned to. Working out as a form of body love is a much nicer energy. Exercising out of love for your body changes everything. It changes how, when and with whom you exercise.

Exercise is a great way of balancing out your 'peopling'. I love people, so going to a gym or a class feels like a treat to me. Mark, my husband, is a major introvert and prefers to work out at home. If you work and live alone, you might benefit from a group exercise activity such as a walking group or a dance class. If you are surrounded by people all day, you might like to exercise alone without anyone annoying you!

My favourite way to move is to dance, moving to music. I have always loved to dance. As a little girl I dreamt of being a ballerina; as a teenager I wanted to be a *Solid Gold* dancer. The closest I got was teaching aerobics! As a born performer, I thought that the performance aspect of dance was what I loved, but I later learnt that my body just loves to move to music. It responds to sound.

Facilitated dance encourages you to move in ways you have never moved before. About 20 years ago I came across a book called *Sweat Your Prayers* by Gabrielle Roth. Gabrielle is the founder of a dance practice called 5Rhythms, which is a dynamic movement practice that ignites your creativity, reconnects you to yourself and takes you beyond self-imposed limitations. It starts with 'Flowing', being fluid, flexible and surrendered. You then move into 'Staccato', a strong, masculine energy with drums, which helps connect your feet with your feelings! 'Chaos' follows. Chaos is big! It is the energy of release and liberation. 'Lyrical' is expansive and expressive. Then comes 'Stillness', a slow motion that eventually leads to lying on the ground.

Gabrielle was a pioneer, and there are now many different forms of dance practice based on her work. I love to attend dance retreats facilitated by a wonderful teacher, where I can immerse myself in the practice of being connected to my body. However, the wonderful thing is that you need no training or equipment – you can get facilitated dance music and dance at home on your own, or you can join classes such as Open Floor or Dancing in the Dark.

I spend a lot of time travelling and have always enjoyed 'dancing in my undies' most mornings. This was a bit of a shock during that pandemic when I was at home 24/7 and my family wondered what was going on!

*

Turn the page to find ideas and suggestions to Get, Guard and Give physical energy.

# Getting physical energy is all about action!

Our physical energy comes from our actions, the things we do daily. Action is what's required. We all know what to do; knowledge is not what we need. We need to take action every day.

Start small. Use technology to support you: timers to tell you to go to bed; habit trackers to keep you on the right path; weekly food delivery to free up time for more important things. What you do is what matters.

- **Daily action:** Initiate your journey towards optimal energy by taking daily actions. Start small, build habits gradually and leverage technology to maintain consistency.
- **Supplement support:** Consider using supplements to complement your diet. Consult with a qualified expert such as a naturopath to identify the right supplements to address your specific nutrient needs.
- **Exercise:** Incorporate regular movement into your life, choosing activities you genuinely enjoy. Exercise boosts physical energy, enhances mood and promotes overall well-being.

# Guarding physical energy is all about habits!

We guard our energy with good habits. Our habits are a means to an end. They help us to help ourselves. The things we do daily are incredibly important when we want to honour our bodies.

We expect our bodies to move, breathe, think, feel, circulate blood and remove waste every day. It makes sense that we need to make a daily effort to help them as well.

As BJ Fogg wrote in *Tiny Habits*, habits 'teach us the skills of change and they propel us towards our dreams, and they add more shine to the world. By embracing feelings of success and adding more goodness to your day-to-day life, you are making the world brighter not only for yourself, but also for others'.

- **Good habits:** Develop and uphold good habits that protect your physical energy. Prioritise daily practices such as movement, good sleep patterns and mindful eating to safeguard your overall well-being.
- **Quality sleep:** Ensure you get both the quantity and quality of sleep required. Aim for seven to nine hours of uninterrupted sleep in a comfortable, dark environment with a supportive mattress and bedding.
- **Closing ceremony:** Create a closing ceremony for your evenings to signal to your body that it's time to wind down. An hour before bedtime, engage in calming activities such as sipping soothing tea, gentle stretching, skincare routines and relaxation through reading or meditation.

## Giving physical energy is all about effort!

Our energy is designed to be given away. Effort is the way we do this. It's about going the extra mile; it's about doing a bit more. Making an effort is about physically showing up, about putting all your physical energy to good work.

Effort looks different for different people. For someone who is struggling, it takes effort to get dressed and leave the house. For someone who is shy, it takes effort to attend a networking event for an hour. What is effort for you? What would stretch you? What would be worth striving for? Who is worth effort in your life?

As Todd Henry wrote in *Die Empty*, 'Embrace the importance of now, and refuse to allow the lull of comfort, fear, familiarity, and ego to prevent you from taking action on your ambitions … The cost of inaction is vast. Don't go to your grave with your best work inside of you. Choose to die empty'.

- **Effort:** Contribute to the world by giving your physical energy through effort. Identify areas where your actions can make a positive impact on relationships, work or community involvement.
- **Turning up:** 'Turn up turned on' is one of my favourite phrases. If you are turning up somewhere, turn yourself on. Bring a plate of energy everywhere you go. Don't turn up energetically empty-handed!

Your body is your most valuable asset. Treat it with care and respect to enjoy the increased vitality and a more fulfilling life.

# 3

# EMOTIONAL ENERGY

*'I want to know if you can disappoint another to be true to yourself.'*

~ Oriah Mountain Dreamer, 'The Invitation'

Our emotional energy comes from how we feel. Emotions are currents of energy that run through us. Think of your emotions as guides: they show you how you feel in any situation. Emotions are the raw data, your reaction to your reality. They are sensations in your body, physiological experiences or states of awareness that give you information about the world.

Feelings are what we make them mean. Feelings are generated from our thoughts about our emotions, from conscious awareness of the emotions themselves.

Humans are meaning-making machines. We make up stories to explain why certain events happen in our lives. Most humans hate uncertainty, so it reassures us to create a story about why something has happened. These stories comfort us even if they are not true. However, more often than not, these stories do not serve us. Say a friend ignores you at an event. You might create a story about how she doesn't like you, how she is no longer your friend. You might even go down a tunnel of all the other people you do not think like you and dig up feelings from the past. But your friend may have been preoccupied or busy and simply not seen you. Your story might be completely untrue. Creating it has caused you unnecessary pain and distress!

Emotions can be stimulated by many things: a thought, an event, a social interaction, a conversation or a memory. We cannot choose the emotions we feel, but we do get to choose our feelings – the ways we respond – through emotional awareness.

Emotional awareness is the ability to recognise and make sense of your emotions. Being in touch with your emotions is a wonderful outcome of knowing yourself. You know what you like and what you don't. You are able to identify and discuss how you are feeling. Being emotionally unaware is exhausting. It's like being in a country where you do not understand the language: you are constantly confused!

Unfortunately, most of us are not very good at experiencing our emotions. We often avoid our feelings as they can be painful and ugly. Who wants to invite pain and ugliness into their lives? No one! From an early age, our emotions were often shut down. We were taught not to cry, that it was not OK to get angry, that feeling jealous meant we were bad people. We were taught that our emotions are our enemies and that we should avoid them at all costs!

However, feelings are a necessary part of being human. The reality is that if you do not access and process your feelings, they will turn up in other ways.

Abraham Maslow's Hierarchy of Needs is a theory of psychological health stating that human needs can be grouped into five tiers, and each tier of needs must be met in order of priority. The first tier, which must be met first, is physiological needs – food, water, shelter, and so on. After our physiological needs are met, safety and security follow, then love and belonging. Being valued and loved and having connection with other humans is incredibly important to us. Only after all these needs are met do we look for higher-order needs such as achievement, respect, creativity and purpose.

Emotionally, people often come unstuck at the second tier: safety. In an effort to feel safe, people often avoid painful, ugly emotions. They push them down or bury them rather than processing them.

Most of us focus more on our external personas than we do on what's happening inside our bodies. When we feel sad, unworthy or unfulfilled on the inside, it shows up externally. We might use substances to mask these feelings, or we might use material objects to create a sense of success and fulfilment. Alcohol, smoking, vaping, shopping and even exercising can all be used to distract us from feeling our feelings.

The worst manifestation of unprocessed feelings is when they show up as disease in our bodies. Louise Hay talks about disease as 'dis-ease'. Dis-ease is the way your body experiences pain. Louise believed that pain, discomfort or negative sensations are caused by emotions that are held within our bodies. When we don't acknowledge and release emotions, dis-ease occurs: 'The body, like everything else in life, is a mirror of our inner thoughts and beliefs. Our body is always talking to us; we just need to take the time to listen.'

I love the personal responsibility of this. I love the idea of discovering how our emotions show up in our bodies. Louise Hay is probably the most significant teacher I have had in my life. While I was lucky enough to meet her once, I have never been personally taught by her, but I have spent the past 30 years swimming in her work, reading, learning and studying everything she has written and said.

## So, what are these emotions that we need to deal with?

There are five emotions featured in the famous children's movie *Inside Out*. Made by Pixar and released in 2015, *Inside Out* is a film about an 11-year-old girl, Riley, who moves cities with her family. It focuses on five personified emotions that administer her thoughts and actions. Director Pete Docter engaged well-known psychologist Paul Ekman, an expert is micro expressions, to create five incredible characters:

1. **Joy** is a light-hearted, optimistic character. She is determined to make everything fun. She sees every challenge in Riley's life as an opportunity.
2. **Fear**'s job is to keep Riley safe. He is always looking ahead for potential problems and is constantly worried about risks! He is always catastrophising everything into the worst possible scenario.
3. **Anger** is very concerned with things being 'fair'. He is very fiery and can't cope when things do not go according to plan. He is super reactive and has zero patience!
4. **Disgust** is super opinionated and brutally honest. She has high standards and is always on the lookout for things that might 'contaminate' Riley's world.
5. **Sadness** finds it hard to be positive! She is mopey and finds it hard to move on. She lives in the past and dwells on what 'could have been'.

Which of these characters do you relate to the most? Allowing yourself to be all of these emotions is really important.

## 1. Joy

Joy can range from amusement to ecstasy. Enjoyment is derived through one of the five senses: it can come from touch when you pat an animal, taste when you eat berries off a vine, smell when you get a whiff of something that triggers a wonderful memory, sight when you see an incredible sunset or hearing when you listen to someone's voice. It can come from experiencing something very funny, witnessing human kindness, celebrating a personal achievement or connecting with a person, animal or place. The best definition of joy for me is like happiness but bigger!

I am a lot like Joy in the movie; people have even commented that we have the same haircut! My kids get annoyed by me constantly reframing things into opportunities and being so optimistic. (Having a motivational speaker for a mother can be very annoying!)

## 2. Fear

Fear is a useful emotion until it is not! Designed to keep us safe, fear stops us from doing dumb or dangerous things. Our fear of danger lets us anticipate threats to our safety. It's OK to be scared – we are all scared. The problem is that fear can create mental paralysis: if you spend too much time with fear, you will end up doing nothing at all! Everything you want is on the other side of fear.

If your level of fear is debilitating or completely irrational, then it is worth getting professional help. Living with large amounts of fear is hard work! Fear is pessimistic. It expects that everything will go wrong. Fear can be your 'small self' keeping you small: your soul wants expansion, but your ego wants to hold you back. While fear is useful and I think you should always acknowledge and appreciate it, your life is in trouble if fear is a permanent state.

I have found fear hard to unpack in my head but very logical on paper. When you write down what you are scared of and why, and all of the possible terrible outcomes that you fear wants you to focus on, suddenly they do not seem so terrible. It's like shining a torch under your bed: there are no monsters!

Checking in with where your fear is coming from is an exercise worth doing. Sit down with fear. Have a meeting. Say, *Hi there, fear. What are you doing here? What do you want me to know?* When fear steps up to the plate for me, I say to it, *I see you and thank you for showing up, fear, but I have decided to go against your advice this time.*

I picture my fear as the character from *Inside Out*. He makes me laugh. I am often reassuring him and sending him away!

The antidote to fear is love. Doing what I love always dissolves fear. We all live on a sliding scale of fear to love. Check in with where you are operating from often. We are born with built-in operating systems created from both love and fear. Both are useful. Both keep us safe. Every decision we make and every thought we have is coming from one of these two sources. Always check in with which feeling you are operating from.

### 3. Anger

Anger can be an ugly emotion. It can be scary and disruptive. I don't think people know how to be angry. We are often not allowed to be angry as children – we get shut down and never get to fully go through the process.

It's OK to be angry! Anger happens when we are blocked from something we want or care about, or are treated unfairly. Common anger triggers include injustice, people we care about getting hurt, other people's anger, getting betrayed or rejected by someone and being lied to.

At its most extreme, anger can be one of the most dangerous emotions because of its potential connection to violence. Anger is an emotion that needs to move up and out. If it is held down or trapped in your body, it becomes pain or deep depression. Finding a way to get anger out of your body safely is essential. You can release anger verbally taking yourself somewhere where you can yell or shout, or physically by stomping, kicking or punching something safe like a pillow or cushion. Writing down or talking out how you feel, why you are angry and where the anger has come from – the root cause – can be a great way to build some awareness of the feeling.

### 4. Disgust

What disgusts us is very personal! We are all offended by different things. Disgust is like a warning sign for what could be offensive or even damaging to us. People are disgusted by bodily functions, cultural customs, food preferences and social behaviours. I am constantly intrigued by what people are disgusted by!

### 5. Sadness

Sadness is useful. It shows us what we care about. Endings, goodbyes and losing people are very common causes of sadness.

A common response is crying. I think crying is underrated. It washes pain away and helps us cleanse. And yet we are so reluctant to cry, even unable. It's not surprising, really, given most of us were stopped when we cried as children. Our emotions got shut down because they made other people uncomfortable, because they weren't socially acceptable. It's no wonder that as adults many of us cannot access or regulate our emotions.

✦

While there are way more emotions than five, these primary emotions are very relatable to many.

The other characters I love in *Inside Out* are Forgetter Bobby and Forgetter Paula, who decided which memories Riley needed to keep (and stored them) and which could be discarded. The movie shows a storeroom of carefully stored emotions. If Riley feels sad, the team runs around looking for an old memory that they can insert into her mind to remind her of a time when she had fun or felt better.

The whole film is a wonderful example of how our minds work, and it had a huge impact on me. Years on, I still consider which emotion is 'running my control desk' several times throughout the day.

Louise Hay distils things down further and teaches that there are really just two emotions that contribute to dis-ease: fear and anger. Anger can show up as impatience, irritation, frustration, criticism, resentment, jealousy or bitterness. Fear can show up as tension, anxiety, nervousness, worry, doubt, insecurity, unworthiness or feeling like you are not good enough. These are all thoughts that poison the body. The mind–body connection is very real and is continuously being proven by science today.

David R Hawkins' Map of Consciousness is another wonderful resource. It is based on the idea that all things are energy, and every energy has a frequency associated with it. The frequency refers to the shape and relative power of whatever you are measuring. I love referring to the Map and noticing at what level I am vibrating at each day.

Emotions can dramatically affect how our energy moves and flows. How we carry emotions in our minds, bodies and hearts can cause us to experience contraction and fear, or expansion and nourishment, all of which is experienced on a cellular level. The Map of Consciousness is an excellent visual to consider the energy you are putting out and the energy that you are absorbing. It makes me consider who I spend time with and what I might be taking on.

## The feeling factory

I think of my heart as a feeling factory. An emotion arrives at the door, and it is my job to greet it and decide what happens to it.

Sometimes a big emotion will barge through the door. It cannot be stopped. The factory needs to stop whatever it had planned that day and deal with this new feeling. There is a lot to process. Dealing with a big emotion is a very physical experience: there can be tears, rapid breathing, clenched hands, nausea, sweating and palpitations. Quickly, we move into our heads, questioning *Why did this happen?* and feeling injustice *(This is unfair)* and disbelief *(I can't believe this is happening!)*.

Each of these energies needs to be dismantled and processed (see figure 2); as Michael A Singer wrote in *The Untethered Soul*, 'The mind is a place where the soul goes to hide from the heart':

1. **Examine:** what am I feeling? Identify the feeling.
2. **Decide:** can I deal with this now? If you are unable to do the emotion justice in the moment, then you can 'box it up' and come back to it when you have the time and space to process it.
3. **Describe:** how am I feeling?
4. **Notice:** where in my body am I feeling this?
5. **Recognise:** when else have I felt this?
6. **Allow:** fall into the feeling.

Avoidance is a very common technique for keeping emotions at bay, but avoiding feelings forever doesn't work. It works for a short time, sometimes, but it is vital to go back and unpack feelings that you have boxed up. Compartmentalisation can be useful but is not a long-term strategy. Unfelt feelings always show up. You can't heal what you don't feel.

Figure 2: dismantling and processing your feelings

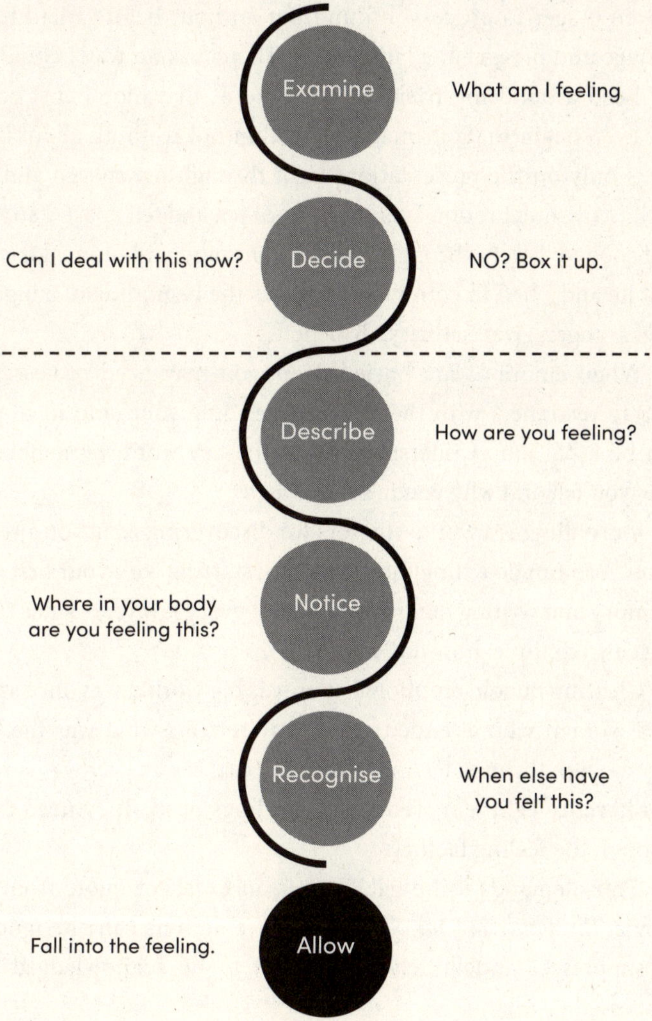

I remember hearing that a good friend of mine had died. It was sudden and a huge shock. His death was a suicide, which made it even bigger to process. I found out an hour before I had to go onstage and present at a large event. There was no way I could get my head around my friend being dead at that moment. I could not even begin to. So, I made a decision not to think about it, to focus only on the presentation. I got through my speech and got back to my hotel room. I made a cup of tea and fell apart. I sobbed and sobbed. I went through all my photos and and phoned friends that he and I had in common. That was the beginning of a big few weeks: anger, grief, sadness, disbelief…

When emotions are buried deep, you may need professional help to reconnect with them. Understanding your emotional past can be a big job. 'Understanding' is the key word: remembering how you felt and why you felt that way.

Journalling is a wonderful tool for discovering what you already know. You can do a timeline of feelings, starting with your first ever memory and writing down how you felt every few years since then. Start at step three: how did you feel?

Clearing out old emotional energy is big work. I was once asked by a woman who attended one of my retreats what was the best way to work through feelings from the past. My answer was simple: you have to feel them. That's what feelings need. They need to go through the feeling factory.

'Pain demands to be felt.' This is an excellent quote from the movie *The Fault In Our Stars*. Painful emotions can't be ignored or suppressed indefinitely; they need to be acknowledged and processed.

The upside of emotional pain is that it cracks us open. When we crack, light gets in. If we constantly hold ourselves just above cracking, we will get very dark.

Letting ourselves fall apart is scary. Often it's not an allowing – it just happens. Incredibly 'tough' people need to allow; they need to let themselves be opened by the can opener of life. You may well have done an excellent job of keeping a lid on your can so far, but it will pop off sooner or later!

## Being comfortable with discomfort

I completely understand why people do not want to know about their emotions. They do not want to experience the pain and the discomfort caused when they step into an emotional space. However, the funny thing about uncomfortable feelings and conversations is that you always feel better on the other side of them. I cannot remember the number of times people have said to me, 'I feel so much better since I had this conversation!'

It is often difficult to label how we are feeling. I love the work of Karla McLaren and her book *The Language of Emotions: What your feelings are trying to tell you.* In it she says, 'What if every feeling – even shame and anxiety – brought you vital information and wisdom? Emotions – especially the unwanted and dishonoured ones – hold a tremendous amount of energy. We've all seen what happens when we repress or recklessly express them.'

Karla worked with her Dynamic Emotional Integration® community to create a list of emotions organised alphabetically by emotion and intensity: karlamclaren.com/product/emotional-vocabulary-fold-out-lists/. This list is genius when it comes to assessing and articulating how and what you are feeling. Using it to identify your emotions and the level of each that you are experiencing helps with awareness. Each of our emotions has a vibration, and if you don't know what it is then it is very hard to become aware of how you are feeling and the impact that this has on your energy and the energy of those around you.

Having regular stillness in your day will create space for your awareness and connection to yourself to grow. It's very hard to hear your feelings while you are running around a supermarket or an office! We often go to stillness when we are feeling overwhelmed or searching for guidance, but it is the everyday quiet that will boost our emotional energy. We need to make space for feeling. Connect to your breath and check in with how you are really feeling. *I am exhausted* might lead you to *I am disappointed*, to *I am really sad*. We need to create the space to feel. We avoid it because we are scared that feeling hurts.

## People placement

Your ability to be at your best is often a result of the people that you spend time with. All of us have an energy vibe, like a personal wi-fi signal that others pick up on. Who are the people that lift you up – your amplifiers, your cheerleaders, the people who believe in you and want the best for you? These people are tank-fillers. Find these people and keep them close. Celebrate with them. Share yourself. Make it your mission to find five great people that add value to your world, people who understand part of your life. They may not understand it all, but they will be perfect for part of it.

I have spent a huge amount of time collecting and curating great people. I love people, and I love being surrounded by people who love, energise and inspire me. I have the most wonderful people in my world. I was recently told that I am lucky, but luck has nothing to do with it. The reason that I have such amazing people in my world is that I am constantly on the lookout for amazing people to add to my carefully curated collection. I put a lot of time into people, understanding and celebrating them. Great friendships don't just happen – you need to make an effort to get good people into your world. Look for them, nurture them and honour them. Get a people plan: decide what type of people your life is lacking, and describe them. What do they enjoy? Where will you find them? When you meet people you enjoy, find ways to spend more time with them.

Having the right people in your life is essential for being loved, understood, supported and extended. Evolutionary psychologist Robin Dunbar suggests that we need five close friends, 15 friends, 50 acquaintances and 150 known names. Sometimes it is a quantity game and sometimes it is a quality issue! To quote another famous Robin, Robin Williams – or, rather, the character he played in the 2009 movie *World's Greatest Dad* – 'I used to think that the worst thing in life was to end up alone. It's not. The worst thing in life is to end up with people who make you feel alone'. I couldn't agree more. Being in a room full of people and feeling alone is a shitty feeling. That is why the game of finding and connecting with new people is so essential. What is your people problem? Not enough people? Or not enough of the right people?

In 1960, PD Eastman wrote a children's book called *Are You My Mother?* It's the story of a baby bird who hatches while his mother is out looking for food, and so he sets off to try and find her. Not knowing what he is looking for, he approaches many different animals and machines asking if they are his mother. I like to play a game with myself in airports and busy streets where I look at everyone coming towards me and imagine asking, 'Are you my friend?' Considering every person walking towards you as a possible friend is a wonderful way to view the world! Trust your gut. (It's an interesting way to explore unconscious bias as well.)

If you're doing a good job of living, then you will be constantly changing. You will be growing, moving and shifting your thinking, your life and your interests. Change is feared by many. Resist it at your peril! As we change, the people we want and need also change.

## Who are your people right now?

When I ask people about their favourite people, I am always met with an automated response. People reply with who they 'should say'. We often feel obligated to state that our partners and families are the people who are adding the most value in our lives at any one time. In my experience this is not always the case. I have had times when I have been working deeply on a project with someone and felt more in touch and like I have more in common with that person than anyone I am living with or related to! I have had these moments in deeply intimate conversations with people I have only just met, or with people I have come together with over a shared passion or experience.

Do you have loads of people in your life who are more like your past than your future? Are they people who you used to have things in common with but you either no longer have those things in common or no longer care about those things?

Think about the type of people you like. Where do they hang out? I know that I'm way more likely to meet someone I connect with at a bookshop or a personal development retreat than at a sports event. Having said that, I met one of my best friends, Fiona, at a post-sporting-event function – we bonded over the fact that neither of us wanted to be there!

You get the picture. Think about who you want in your life and where these people are likely to be found, and then go out and see if you can find them.

Think about the facets of your life. I am a multifaceted maximalist. I am a creative, opinionated businesswoman who adores alternative views and modalities and believes deeply in the divinity of the universe.

I have creative friends – people who are always making, drawing, painting, cooking or stitching something. I have opinionated friends – people who stand for things; I do not have to share their beliefs, but I love their commitments to causes and issues. I have business friends – people who love commercial conversations and are constantly creating and testing new products and ideas. I have alternative friends – people who live off the grid, who adore nature and use it to sustain their bodies and minds. I have universal friends – people who celebrate their god selves and are obsessed with awareness and consciousness.

What are your friend categories? What vacancies do you have?

As well as different types of interests, we also need different types of energy. We need supportive friends – people who fan our flames, who are never far away with a 'good for you', 'you're amazing' or 'you've got this'. We need helpful friends – people who turn up, who reach out, who lean in. I call these people 'contributors'. Quite simply, they add value, either by being useful, kind, supportive or just fun. You feel great when you are with them and enjoy their company.

Who is contributing to your life? Appreciate these people and do kind things for them. I'm a big birthday card person. If you value someone in your life, think about how you can honour them by making sure that you are contributing back. How do you say, 'Thank you for making a difference in my life'?

## Dealing with contaminators

The opposite of contributors are 'contaminators'. These people weigh you down. They muddy your waters and make you feel yucky. Your vibration drops merely by being in their presence. You feel shitty after you've been with them.

An easy way to identify a contaminator is that your bum goes tight when you're around them! If your phone rings and you recognise the number, but you don't answer because you don't want to talk to that person, they're a contaminator. If you see someone in the supermarket and want to run the other way, they're a contaminator. Sometimes you don't know why; sometimes it's a vibe. I find I am uncomfortable with people who are uncomfortable in themselves. I pick up on their energy, and it impacts mine.

Some people need to put others down to feel good about themselves: mothers who comment on their daughter's weight, daughters who talk about their mother's clothes, sisters who judge your husband, and so on. This is called 'levelling'. A person who puts you down, belittles you or who does not have your best interests at heart is not a friend; they are an energy robber. They ring you up, talk about themselves, whinge, whine and moan, and then hang up the phone. You are left feeling like a deflated balloon with one less hour in your day!

Think about who's contributing to your life and who's contaminating it. You will find that every single person in your life, whether they are your children, colleagues, partner, friends or family, is either contributing or contaminating. If they are contaminating, it may not be their fault – they might be unwell or dealing with difficult stuff. They might be teenagers! Nevertheless, be aware of these people. As a good friend, you will want to be there for them, but it shouldn't be at the expense of yourself. Supporting people is not easy. You need to give yourself space and grace and permission to step away every now and then.

Sometimes people need to be removed from or repositioned in our lives. Mentally shifting people off to the side can be very important for your well-being. Moving away from negative, dramatic or nasty people is self-protection. We all have people in our lives who are messing with our energy. Sometimes they are temporary people, such as someone you are working with. Sometimes these people come free with your life like a set of cheap steak knives – they are in your family or are legally attached in some way. Sometimes they are your partner or children. Having a strategy to deal with these people is essential, but you need to identify and acknowledge who they are before you can deal with them!

Have a look at table 1 overleaf and see what names pop into your head.

The problem with all of these people is that they have no awareness. They are all fighting for attention, control, status, relief, power and sympathy. Your job is to notice. Know who these people are in your life and be on red alert.

Table 1: contaminators

| | |
|---|---|
| **The Drama Queen**<br>**Want:** Attention<br>**Issue:** Adrenalin<br>**Need:** Awareness | These people are dramatic 24/7. They burn your energy with all their huffing and puffing and trashing around. They overexaggerate and have dramatic reactions to things that happen. Unconsciously, they want attention. They don't want their problems solved – as soon as their problems are solved, they head straight out looking for new ones. |
| **The Human Dumpster**<br>**Want:** Relief<br>**Issue:** Overwhelm<br>**Need:** Reflection | These people vomit their problems all over you with regular toxic venting. They are desperate to dump the yucky feelings they are carrying around onto you! They are heavier than the Drama Queen, more negative. They don't want to take any responsibility for their lives. They have no interest in whether what they are sharing is relevant, helpful, accurate or even of interest to you; they just have to 'get it out'. |
| **The Control Freak**<br>**Want:** Power<br>**Issue:** High expectations<br>**Need:** Awareness | These people are holding on tightly and cannot work out why life is so torturous. They are white-knuckling everything. Controlling and judging are their favourite things to do. To bring a sense of safety to their worlds, they want to control as much as they can! |
| **The Virtuous Victim**<br>**Want:** Sympathy<br>**Issue:** Blame<br>**Need:** Power | Everything happens 'to' these people. They have zero agency and are always complaining about what someone has 'done to them'. They always have someone who is treating them unfairly or large problems that never seem to be fixed. |
| **The Mighty Narcissist**<br>**Want:** Attention<br>**Issue:** Superiority<br>**Need:** Admiration | These people require constant praise and admiration. They think that they are special. They are quick to anger if things don't go their way. They are extremely self-involved and have very little concern for the needs of those around them. |

You know who these people are in your world: the friends who only call when they want something; the people who drain you; the people who you know before you spend time with them will have a negative impact on your energy. These people are human barnacles that attach to you. You will be surprised how empowering it is to make a list of these people in your life and write down a strategy for dealing with each of them. You have taken back the power and are now energetically in charge!

Have a strategy for each one:

- Stay very calm around **the Drama Queen**. Don't buy into any of their drama. Respond with, 'That must be difficult'.
- Limit your time and availability around **the Human Dumpster**. Say, 'I'm not in a space to do this right now'.
- Hold your ground with **the Control Freak**. Say, 'Thanks for your idea, but I'm going to do it differently'.
- Don't offer sympathy or advice to **the Virtuous Victim**. Ask, 'What can you do about that?'
- Keep your distance from **the Mighty Narcissist**. Create space. These people are master manipulators.

My friend Lesley is a wonderful therapist and the best person to have a conversation with. Years ago, Lesley taught me about catching energy balls: 'Sometimes people throw us balls, instinctively we catch them. Without realising it a transfer of energy has occurred. We are left holding the negative feelings of the interaction. We hang onto this and it becomes another burden to carry.'

Once I became aware of these energy balls, I was able to decide for each whether I was going to catch it, dodge it, put it down or carry it around with me. It became a conscious choice.

Walking into a conversation with a Human Dumpster can be like having a tennis ball fired at you at high speed – you have to be ready! Narcissists have a wonderful knack for making you feel terrible, manipulating you into feeling like something is your fault, and that can feel like a bowling ball to the stomach.

We all have parts of these personalities in ourselves. Everyone has the ability to be a bit controlling, to vent in an unhealthy way, to be dramatic. A moderate degree of narcissism is normal and can be healthy in humans with self-awareness. But people who make these behaviours their life theme are very difficult to be around. Doing the work required to have great energy is a lot, and you cannot risk a drainer or a dumper coming in and destroying your efforts!

Being with these people can make you feel hideous until you don't allow it. You have two choices: either restrict your contact with the person or tell them that they have no right to speak to you like that. You need to teach people how to treat you. Decide what you will and won't accept. I had a friend during the pandemic who seemed to have a constant flow of problems. She was the only one, of course! I turned our conversations into a game where she was allowed to select three problems each day to discuss. Of course, she would get on a roll and launch into a fourth topic, and I would laugh and say, 'Time's up! That's all we have time for today!'

Staying light in heavy situations is an amazing tool to master. Making the decision to stay light is powerful. It means that you respond rather than react. It means that you stay in your power, managing yourself and responding in a way that you want to.

Another one of my favourite tools is to find humour in any situation. Every time you find humour in a difficult situation, you win. I have a natural ability to find things funny. I am able to spring to a funny or optimistic view even of terrible, tragic things. You can choose to be Eeyore, heavy and sad, or you can be optimistic Winnie the Pooh – or go even further to bouncy Tigger!

As a result of having children later in life, many people are now finding themselves in 'The sandwich generation': middle-aged adults who care for both their aging parents and their own children. This can be incredibly challenging and energy-draining. If this is you, you need a strategy. Write a list of all the people in your world. Write down what's difficult about them and what they need from you. Brainstorm who else can help. What support services are available to you? Learn to ask for help and find someone who you can debrief with. Being a caregiver is big work. You need to care for yourself so you can care for other people.

I've got four children, and at any one time, one or more of them can be contributing or contaminating. They can go from one to the other very quickly – especially teenagers! They are not aware of the enormous amount of energy they have. They are often moody and are constantly in a state of flux, which causes all kinds of odd behaviour. My children are some of the best humans I know, I adore them, but there are times when I have wanted to put each of them in the wheelie bin. They have all gone through challenging phases and can go from being my favourite humans on the planet to the most annoying! The trick has been to stay light and know that nothing is forever. 'Everything is a phase' was one of the most helpful mantras I had when my kids were younger.

One of the best strategies I have learnt for dealing with challenging children comes from a wonderful New Zealand psychologist and author called Nigel Latta, who has written a number of excellent parenting books. He has developed a character called Mad Uncle Jack (or Mad Auntie Jane if you are looking for a female version), a wonderful invention to help parents not take things personally when their teenagers act badly. In *The Politically Incorrect Guide to Teenagers*, he asks you to imagine asking Mad Uncle Jack if he'd like a cup of tea only for him to call you a bitch and storm off:

> 'Now, would you let that ruin your evening or would you just think: "Ah well, it's Uncle Jack being mad again, no surprises there"? Would you wonder if mad old pee-smelling Uncle Jack had a point? Would you start to question yourself? No. So why would you get upset when your son or daughter does the same thing?'

Think, too, about who or what *you* have contaminated. Think back to when you did something wrong, when you let someone down or stuffed something up. Maybe you told someone a lie? I find that these things follow us energetically. I use the analogy of poo in the swimming pool. I remember as a kid that when someone had pooed in the pool, the more I tried to get away from the dreaded poo, the faster it seemed to chase me. I feel the same about the mistakes I make with other people! They keep floating along behind me until I resolve them. I need to scoop them out and deal with them!

I check in every week with my energy pool. Dealing with shits as they arrive is far better than leaving them to pile up!

## Do a people audit

I regularly audit the people in my world. Who is right for right now? Making a list of the types of people you need, who is contributing and who is contaminating, is an exercise worth doing regularly. We all need people. We are wired to connect. Taking responsibility for the number, quality and type of people in our lives is important.

Every person in your life is like a browser tab on your computer. Who do you have browser tabs open for?

- **Your constants:** your nearest and dearest, the people who have come free with your life. These are your family, neighbours and oldest friends.
- **Your project people:** people who are in your life for a reason or a season. You might be involved in a project with them; they might be friends.
- **The casuals:** the people who you bump into and interact with in the course of daily life. They could be the doctor's receptionist or the man who mows your lawns. You may never get to know them, but they can have an impact on your energy.

Each tab takes up energy. I frequently check in with what tabs I have open. Tabs that remain open are like leaving the fridge door ajar: they are a waste of energy! Open tabs could include someone you haven't got back to, someone you promised something to or someone who owes you something. These are all little energy loops using up energy that you often are not consciously aware of.

I use journalling to bring awareness to these people. Who am I holding space for? Who do I have old loops open with? Who do I need to tidy up?

Listing all the people who are in your space and how you feel about them is a great way to check in with your energetic balance. Are you caring for too many people? You may not be caring for them directly, but if they are anywhere in your circle of concern then you are holding space for them. They are taking up space on your energetic hard drive.

It's worth putting in the effort to close these tabs. Close down the energy loops you don't need to be holding space for. Get back to that person. Fulfil that promise. Call in that debt. This is essential for good energy management.

## Long-term relationships

A good relationship will add enormous value to your world, but the wrong relationship will be a drain. It's worth keeping in mind that even in a good relationship, one third of the things your partner is and does you will love, one third will drive you completely mad (like how they don't put their washing in the basket or replace the toilet roll) and one third won't bother you and you may not even notice at all. Long-term relationships require work, they need tolerance and space, and they need room for growth and change.

I have two friends whose husbands left them – both suddenly and both for other women. One of them understands that while it was incredibly sad, disruptive and traumatic at the time, their relationship had stagnated. They have both now moved on to new, fulfilling relationships, and they get on great and co-parent together. My other friend decided that her husband left her because she wasn't good enough, that she needed to be better. She made her relationship breakdown her fault due to her not being thin enough. She is now obsessed with healthy eating, barely talks about anything except food and exercise, and has no social life. Rather than process what happened, she has distracted herself with a project.

We all have wounds – from childhood, from relationships. We all have fear in our hearts. Our life is a series of experiences, some good and some bad. It's not what happens to us that's the problem – it is what we make it mean. Carl Jung wrote in *The Undiscovered*

*Self*, 'We should not pretend to understand the world only by the intellect; we apprehend it just as much by feeling. Therefore, the judgment of the intellect is, at best, only the half of truth, and must, if it be honest, also come to an understanding of its inadequacy'. Intellect is important, but you must respect your feelings!

A few years ago I heard spiritual author Neale Donald Walsch speak. He said, 'I want you to go home and tell your partner, "Thank you for witnessing my life".' I love that! I thought that was really powerful. He reckons thousands of people go through their days with no one to notice them. It's really affirming to have someone who recognises that you're in a bad mood or that you haven't had a good day, or someone who knows that you just got promoted and that something has gone right – even someone to see that you just bought new shoes.

## The lickable third

In my book *The Lickable Third* (2018), I wrote about making your life 33% better. The book is based upon a game my brother and I played as children where we licked things we wanted or loved as a sign of ownership, such as the biggest scone freshly out of the oven, a piece of chocolate on a plate or the biggest piece of fish in a pile of fish and chips! The lickable stuff in your life is the best stuff. Removing the non-lickable stuff will improve everything. I reckon that's about one third of everything in your life: one third of the people, the stuff, the clothing… of every area of your world.

The theory is very simple: one third of your life is brilliant, one third is OK and one third is shit! Your life is precious; it is special and irreplaceable. We are all here for a limited time, so we need to be ruthless with our lives. The lickable third is about being discerning: it's about saying 'no' to the things that don't matter so you can say 'yes' to the things that do. As personal finance expert Nathan W Morris wrote in *Your 33 Day Money Action Plan*, 'Edit your life frequently and ruthlessly. It's your masterpiece after all'.

In our busy, overstuffed and overwhelmed modern world, the secret to having loads of emotional energy to share with your people is to do more with less. Spend more time with your most favourite people. Wear your favourite clothes every day.

You need to focus on the things that you love about yourself, the people in your life and the things you own. Imagine you have three rooms:

1. Room one is where you put all of the people that drive you nuts, all of the clothes that you never wear and all the stuff you have been given but didn't want. You get to fill this room with everything that you do not like and wish was gone.
2. Room two is a holding pen for the stuff you are not sure about: the clothes and other things that you don't love but are practical, and the people who aren't your favourite but you do not dislike either.
3. Room three is your trophy room, the space to showcase all your best stuff: your nicest clothes, your best friends and the best people you have ever worked with and the most beautiful cups and plates that you own.

Which room would you like to spend the most time in? Imagine only living in room three!

The section of your life you spend the most time in is a decision. Being discerning is about having fewer people, less stuff, more time and more happiness! You have limited time and energy, so stop wasting it on people who do not add value to your life.

## 'No' is a full sentence

I am a recovering people-pleaser. As an eldest daughter and self-proclaimed 'good girl', I have invested a lot of time into, and placed a lot of importance on, being liked.

Pleasing people did, and still does, make me happy. I love to see people's faces light up when I deliver a gift, a project or an event. I love the feeling of people being 'happy with me', being 'pleased'. But people-pleasing is a shitty currency, and many of us trade in it without realising!

What are you liked for? We are taught from an early age to please and what to care about. The things that we were rewarded for as children often show up in our adult behaviours: being on time, being polite, looking smart, minimising our behaviour, sitting quietly and being fucking patient! Desperate to be 'seen' or just 'noticed', we set out to please everyone and often end up selling out on who we truly are.

As an opinionated, extroverted show pony, being seen and not heard and only speaking when I was spoken to took enormous effort! It was soul-destroying. By the age of 30 I realised that I could not play the game anymore. I made the decision that being myself was more important to me than being liked, and I was no longer going to compromise myself for the comfort of others.

But it crept back. In any new situation, any new level of my life, the need to please became a form of insurance. It was useful – until it wasn't.

People-pleasers spread themselves as thin as marmite! So eager to make others happy, they blurt out, 'Of course!' and, 'Yes! No problem!' before it even occurs to them to say, 'I can't right now', or, 'No, thanks'. It's like they created an auto-reply 20 years ago and the coding has stuck.

We take responsibility for other people's reactions. We feel bad when others feel bad, and we try to minimise any discomfort to those around us. Over-responsibility is a huge problem. We tend to take a ridiculous amount of responsibility for whether or not people are having a good time, so much so that we completely forget that *us* enjoying ourselves is even an option.

The root cause of people-pleasing is a healthy dose of 'I'm not good enough' with a side salad of 'I don't matter'. People-pleasing is rooted in fear. We want people to like us. We are happy to give up our comfort in an effort to make others comfortable. We spend way too much time worrying about how our choices or needs might impact or inconvenience others. Instead of asking the people in our lives for what we need and desire, we say no for them! We decide to settle for a role as a background character in other people's stories. I am here to tell you that you are the main character. Enough of this back-seat shit!

If you are still reading, you can bet that you are a caring, capable and committed person:

- **You care deeply about people.** You probably have a shit ton of people in your paddock – people who rely on you for something. You have a radar for what people need: whether it's something to eat, some advice or a listening ear, you intuitively know what is needed in most situations.
- **You are capable.** Not only do you do a lot, you do it effortlessly, minimising your greatness and not causing too much of a scene! You have initiative and are a get-shit-done kind of human, constantly frustrated by how other people can be so ineffective!

- **You are committed.** You pride yourself on getting things done, on turning up, on being there – wherever 'there' is!

There are many places people-pleasing can come from. I am a big fan of moving forward, so rather than focus on all the reasons we develop the disease to please, I am more interested in what we can do about it! As the famous Dr Phil said, 'You can't fix what you don't acknowledge'. Acknowledging is the first step to awareness.

Here's what to do:

- **Stop.** Breathe. Remove your auto-response. Catch yourself and create some space between people's requests and your reply.
- **Ask.** Is this really something I want to do? You need to be the first person you check in with. Make your opinion the most important opinion in your life.
- **Listen.** Listen to yourself. Listen to your instincts. Spend more time alone so you can hear your inner voice without the clatter of other people's needs, wants and distractions.
- **Prioritise.** Be intentional about what you are and aren't doing. Be clear about what you are and are not available for. Run your day so the day doesn't run you!

Learning how to turn people down is an energetic game changer! As Marianne Williamson once said, 'Love is always the answer but sometimes love says "No"'.

I love the concept that 'no' is a full sentence. I find it useful to visualise myself saying no to people. I have practised saying no! I love to practise saying things out loud when I'm driving. It's a wonderful way to get yourself used to saying the things you think might be difficult to say to someone else. These sentences are useful:

'I am going to have to say no.'

'I have other things I am focused on right now.'

'That sounds like heaven, but it's not right for me right now.'

'I would love to, but…'

Overgiving is a problem that many of us have: we give and love and help and end up completely depleted because we have not put the right support around ourselves. Giving at the expense of ourselves is never a good idea. Oriah Mountain Dreamer is an author and poet I am a huge fan of, and her poem 'The Invitation' changed my life.

***The Invitation***

*It doesn't interest me what you do for a living.*

*I want to know what you ache for and if you dare to dream*
*of meeting your heart's longing.*

*It doesn't interest me how old you are.*

*I want to know if you will risk looking like a fool for love for*
*your dream for the adventure of being alive.*

*It doesn't interest me what planets are squaring your moon...*

*I want to know if you have touched the centre of your own*
*sorrow if you have been opened by life's betrayals or have*
*become shrivelled and closed from fear of further pain.*

*I want to know if you can sit with pain mine or your own*
*without moving to hide it or fade it or fix it.*

*I want to know if you can be with joy mine or your own if you can dance with wildness and let the ecstasy fill you to the tips of your fingers and toes without cautioning us to be careful to be realistic to remember the limitations of being human.*

*It doesn't interest me if the story you are telling me is true.*

*I want to know if you can disappoint another to be true to yourself.*

*If you can bear the accusation of betrayal and not betray your own soul.*

*If you can be faithless and therefore trustworthy.*

*I want to know if you can see beauty even when it is not pretty every day.*

*And if you can source your own life from its presence.*

*I want to know if you can live with failure yours and mine and still stand at the edge of the lake and shout to the silver of the full moon, "Yes."*

*It doesn't interest me to know where you live or how much money you have.*

*I want to know if you can get up after the night of grief and despair weary and bruised to the bone and do what needs to be done to feed the children.*

*It doesn't interest me who you know or how you came to be here.*

*I want to know if you will stand in the centre of the fire with me and not shrink back.*

*It doesn't interest me where or what or with whom you have studied.*

*I want to know what sustains you from the inside when all else falls away.*

*I want to know if you can be alone with yourself and if you truly like the company you keep in the empty moments.*

~ Oriah Mountain Dreamer



My favourite line is, 'I want to know if you can disappoint another to be true to yourself.' How often do you honour the request of someone else and let yourself down? How often do you put the needs of others ahead of your own needs?

Being in service is a wonderful way to live, but I can tell you from experience that if you sacrifice yourself to the point of physical, mental or emotional exhaustion, no one benefits! Saying 'yes' to meeting everyone else's needs and not meeting your own is not smart. Asking for help, getting support and prioritising fun is super smart.

## Get some support

None of us was created to do life on our own. As humans, we were designed to support each other. We are social beings who need others to enhance our lives. The interesting thing about modern living is that we have become unhelpfully independent. We have become crazy, capable, stressed-out little islands who have lost the ability to ask for help or even notice when help is required!

My husband and I still live in the small town that we grew up in. We get asked all the time why we have never moved. Raising our children close to their grandparents was very important to us. Being working parents of four children, we knew that we were going to need some help, so it was a deliberate plan. It is still working now that our parents are getting older and we are able to offer them the support that they once offered us.

An imbalance of help in your world will cause you problems. I recently ran a workshop for 100 busy professional women. When I asked them to write a list of the people who they support, most of them came up with about 15 names: friends, family, children and neighbours all who relied on them for something. When I asked the same group of women to list the number of people who support them, they came up with fewer than five. The difference in these numbers shocked them. No wonder they were feeling stressed out and unsupported! So, who supports you?

Most women in the world aren't getting enough support. This is a huge problem. Women are born supporters. We support everybody. In traditional roles, wives supported husbands. As parents, or as our own parents age, the buck usually stops with us. We get chucked into all the support roles. There are just so many people to support!

It's really, really important that you think about the roles you have in your life where you need support. Are you caring for a sick family member? Do you need to ring another sibling and say, 'It's about bloody time you took your turn'? Do you need someone to drive your kids to school in the morning because you're always late for work, because they go to school on the opposite side of town? Really simple shit like that will change your life.

Years ago, I met a wonderful woman called Marg Culy. She is a life coach and she taught me about creating 'an opportunity to give'. An opportunity to give is the simple offering of allowing others to help you. We often love to help other people, we are honoured when others ask us for help, and yet we find asking for help so difficult. We do not feel like it is OK to ask someone to do something for us, even though it's fine for every other bugger to ask us!

Marg suggested that I phone my friend and tell her that I had a wonderful opportunity for her. I'd say to her, 'I would like to offer you the opportunity to spend four hours with my children on Saturday night. Wouldn't that be amazing?!' And she'd start laughing, and she'd say, 'Yes, that would be amazing. Thank you for that opportunity'. Then, two days later, she'd phone me and say, 'Hey, guess what? I have got this amazing opportunity for you! I just thought it would be wonderful if you picked up my kids after school on Wednesday and gave them dinner'.

I thought that would be amazing! It completely changed the way I asked for help. It was funny and fun, and it gave others permission to ask you in the same way. Genius. So, you're going to have to ring up your friends and tell them that you have learnt about this new opportunity. It is such a nice way of asking for help.

When thinking about where you need support, it's really important that you do not judge yourself. We can all come up with 100 reasons why we do not deserve the support we need, but this is really just self-sabotage. You don't need to be judging yourself, because everyone else is doing that for you. If you want support, you should get it. Easy.

## Filling up with fun

We get emotional energy from many sources. The best source is positive emotions: things that feel good.

Imagine that you are exhausted, you are physically tired and grumpy, but then your phone rings and it is someone telling you that have you have just won a three-week trip to Europe with your four favourite people. The only catch is that you only have two hours to get to the airport. The energy from the thrill of the win and the excitement of the trip would far outweigh your physical tiredness. That's the power of emotional energy. You would no longer be feeling tired and grumpy. You would be lit up. Your heart would be racing. You would be feeling lucky, excited and joyful.

What's the point of working hard if you aren't having any fun? I am big on fun and think it is actually the whole point of life. We are born, we have fun and then we die. I have had many arguments defending this belief! What else is the point? Working well to live well is a wonderful way to live. Collecting experiences and doing things that I love are very high on my priority list. There is nothing else you can take with you when you leave than the experiences you have collected.

I took my four adult children to see Billie Ellish in concert in Auckland. It was an amazing performance and an amazing weekend. It wasn't easy! I have created four individuals with different preferences and personalities who aren't afraid of sharing their thoughts, so it was an opinion-packed few days! But it was fun, and it was an experience. They got to experience Auckland. They got to experience each other, and I got to experience them. It was expensive, but I believe that money is for spending – I would gladly swap cash for experiences. It's a privilege to be able to work hard and play hard, and I am constantly grateful for it.

Doing fun stuff keeps you interesting. It gives you better stories. Where have you been? Who have you met? What have you done? 'Interesting' keeps your energy fresh. Being 'up to something' gives you a very magnetic energy to be around. It makes you energetically attractive! It makes you nicer to work with, live with and be with.

Doing fun stuff is important, but you will notice that it doesn't just happen. It is easy to find yourself bumping along, looking after everyone, attending meetings and doing all the stuff you should do and none of the stuff you want to do – the stuff that you really enjoy. Fun is something you need to plan. Each month, I make sure I have something in my planner that makes me happy, no matter how big or small – something that I can look forward to. It takes the dreariness out of my world and creates a consistent state of enjoyment. Doing more fun stuff is essential when you are busy because it's usually the first thing to go. We get stressed when we do what other people want. Doing more of what we want keeps us buoyant during busy times.

We tend to fill up the wrong tanks. You need more of you. You need to tell the world that you matter. The problem with giving everything to others, with putting other people first, is that we teach them that we come second.

Energy comes from so many sources. Our emotional energy is often enough to get us through those times when our physical energy is compromised. Unfortunately, we are not able to have glorious and constant surprises of winning trips, so how can you find emotional energy in your everyday life? Here are some ideas for how you can fill the right tanks and, as author Sylvester McNutt put it, 'Add value to your own life first'.

## Cultivate passion

Having things in your life that you are passionate about will give you loads of energy, making you leap out of bed, eager to start your day. You know how it feels when you're looking forward to a special event? Passionate people feel like that every day. The combination of passion and good health will give you a high-energy life.

## Have something to look forward to

The power of having something to look forward to can keep people alive – literally! A concert, an event, a holiday, a hobby or people coming to visit are all things that we look forward to. Planning out your year and popping in things that you can get excited about will increase your emotional energy no end.

## Surround yourself with things that make you happy

Dopamine decorating is a real thing! Filling your home, office or room with colour, textures and patterns that bring you joy makes your environment feel inspired. This can look different for everyone, which means the design possibilities are endless. There's no right or wrong way to do it. The only challenge comes from living with other people and compromising when you have different ideas about what looks good.

Feng shui principles teach us that all of our 'things' hold energy. If you have things in your environment that annoy you, they will upset your energy. As 19th-century British designer William Morris said, 'Have nothing in your houses that you do not know to be beautiful or believe to be useful'.

## Wear what makes you happy

You will be surprised by how much what you wear can impact your energy. I spent 20 years working as a stylist. I have always loved transforming people, and helping them to feel good about how they looked was very rewarding. Too many people restrict what they wear because they do not like attention, they do not like their bodies or they are concerned with what other people will say or think. I love the saying that what other people think of you is none of your business. Wearing what you want will give you way more energy and emotional delight than being held to someone else's rulebook.

I love getting dressed. Every day, I wake up excited to decorate myself. I feel like my clothes pick me rather than the other way around. I am led to whatever catches my eye, and then I add a practical lens based on where I am going or what I am doing. Making an effort to gift-wrap yourself each day is a wonderful way to lift your energy.

We have all had the experience of putting on something that changes the way we feel. Feelings are a hugely important part of dressing. Think of how you want to feel emotionally: pretty, smart, organised, creative, important? Also, how do you want to feel physically: warm, soft, contained, structured?

The fabrics, colours and textures you choose all have an impact on how you feel. Your body absorbs the colours that you wear. Your skin responds to the fabrics that you choose. Adorn your body with things that you love. Honour yourself and dress accordingly.

Think about your favourite item of clothing. Describe it. What do you love about it? How does it make you feel? What is it made of? People fall into one of two categories with clothing: function or form. People who prize function will want things that are fit for purpose. They will want things that 'work'. People who prize form will want things that look good. They will ditch comfort over style or design any day. It doesn't matter what you like to wear; what matters is how you feel!

## Change something!

They say that a change is as good as a holiday and making a change will certainly create some emotional energy. Contrary to our beliefs, we all have the ability to completely reinvent ourselves at any time. You can do what you want. It may not feel like it, but you can. Decide who and what you want to be. Change your job, change your location, change your hair. Decide what you want, believe you can have it, work out what you need and take some action.

Action feels good and keeps the darkness away. When I need a boost of emotional energy, I do something. I shift some furniture. I paint something. Occasionally, I clean something! (I'm not a huge fan of cleaning!)

## Do something new

One of the pieces of advice I give out most often is to 'do more'. People are horrified! They are already feeling stressed, overwhelmed and stretched; it doesn't seem very clever to add more. The reason I am so keen on people adding more is that they need to do more of the things that light them up. They are doing too much, but not enough of the things that excite them.

What have you always wanted to do? Where have you always wanted to go? What did you love doing as a child? We become adults and lose touch with what makes us feel good, what we enjoy. Do more of what you love. Do new things. Being a beginner is so good for us. Post-pandemic my friend Charlotte and I were bored, so we made a pact to do something creative each month, something new.

We did resin art. We learnt a lot about ourselves and each other – it turns out I am quite bossy! We did glassblowing workshops. I was obsessed with glassblowing as a child and collected little glass animals. Spending a whole day in a glass foundry and coming home with a funny, wonky bowl was brilliant. I had to follow instructions, listen and do as I was told! None of those things are easy for me.

As adults, we get too comfortable. We become know-it-alls. Learning something new will challenge you and give you new energy.

## Be selfish

People are exhausted. They are 'soul tired': tired of trying, tired of being disappointed, tired of feeling misunderstood. You might think you are stuck, that you are unmotivated. After being in survival for so long, most of us feel depleted.

And the answer is selfishness! It's time to be selfish. It's time to stop self-sacrificing.

I heard a story recently about a woman who walked out on her life. She was 76 years old. She packed a bag and left. It suddenly occurred to her that she was not on this planet forever and that she was not living – she was existing! She no longer wanted the life she had been tolerating. She had been excessively self-sacrificing, giving everything to others and sacrificing her own needs. It was well and truly time for her to be selfish.

Selfishness is probably the last thing you want to identify with. When I wrote my first book, *Look Gorgeous, Be Happy*, I did a lot of research into the word 'selfish'. It confused me because the suffix 'ish' means to be associated with a person or thing. If I am described as 'boyish' it means I am like a boy. If I am described as 'blue-ish' then I am a bit blue. So, my conclusion was that being selfish meant I was 'like me'. Based on those examples, I am very happy to be selfish.

I realised years ago that I needed to be more of myself to cope. With four children and two businesses, it would have been very easy to drown, but me drowning served no one, and the only person who could keep my head up was me. The only person who could give my kids a happy mother was me.

I realised that I deserved the same time, love and energy that I was giving to so many people. I deserved time on my own. I deserved to go to places that lit me up, to spend time with people who inspired me. It was best for everyone. It meant that I was better for my family, for my clients and for my team.

*

Turn the page to find ideas and suggestions to Get, Guard and Give emotional energy.

# Getting emotional energy is all about inspiration!

Inspiration is what give us our emotional energy. When we are lit up by something, we are energised.

- **Get inspired:** Take time to tap into what lights you up, what fills your cup and floats your boat. When you are inspired, it's like being led around by an invisible thread: you feel a pull to do things, to get involved in stuff. It's your job to inspire yourself. Go searching for something amazing that flicks on your switches!
- **Be selfish:** Take time to ponder your desires and interests. Then, make a conscious effort to include activities you enjoy in your life. Create moments of stillness for self-reflection and connecting with your emotions.
- **Seek and accept support:** Understand that you don't have to navigate life's challenges alone. Reach out to others for assistance when necessary. Be open to receiving support and build a supportive community around you. Recognise that asking for help is a sign of strength.

# Guarding emotional energy is all about boundaries!

Good energy is a decision. Decide what you will and will not tolerate. Decide what is and is not OK. Write a memorandum for yourself – the rules of you!

- **Practise saying no:** Build the confidence to say 'no' to requests or commitments that don't align with your goals or priorities. Embrace the idea that 'no' is a complete sentence, and don't feel guilty for declining.
- **Identify energy drains:** Conduct a people audit to assess who you are providing energy to and who supports you in return. Recognise the importance of balanced relationships and set boundaries where needed.
- **Avoid people-pleasing:** Acknowledge the habit of people-pleasing and take steps to break free from it. Stop automatically saying 'yes' and consider your own needs and desires first. Listen to your instincts and be intentional about what you commit to.

## Giving emotional energy is all about enthusiasm!

American self-improvement pioneer Paul Meyer said, 'Enthusiasm is the yeast that rises the dough'. The word 'enthusiasm' comes from Greek and means to have 'god inside' – 'en' meaning 'in' and 'thus' coming from 'theos', which means 'god'. Walking around like you have a god inside you will change your day!

- **Plan fun activities:** Make fun and enjoyable experiences a priority in your life. Schedule regular activities that bring you joy and fulfilment. Remember that life is about collecting meaningful experiences for yourself and others.
- **Set yourself up for success:** Ensure you have the necessary resources for a balanced and fulfilling life, including proper sleep, nutrition and an excellent work environment.

- **Create opportunities to give:** Encourage a reciprocal exchange of support. Offer others the opportunity to help you, just as you are willing to assist them. It can change the dynamics of giving and receiving.

By implementing these actions in your life, you can effectively manage your emotional energy, maintain balance and ensure you're not overextending yourself while still supporting those around you.

# 4

# MENTAL ENERGY

*'Thoughts are mental energy; they're the currency that you have to attract what you desire. You must learn to stop spending that currency on thoughts you don't want.'*

~ Wayne Dyer

People often ask me, 'What is mental energy?' Everyone seems to understand physical, emotional and even spiritual energy, but mental energy seems to need some explaining.

Mental energy comes from our thoughts. My usual explanation is that mental energy is the stuff that stops you going mental!

Most of the problems in the outside world are caused by people not feeling good on the inside, people dealing with all of the mental traps that their minds create: the anxiety, the disturbance and the stress. Lacking concentration, overthinking and feeling bored or understimulated are all symptoms of bad mental energy.

Our minds are tricky places, and if your mental energy is not great then life can be incredibly difficult. Feeling like you 'have your head together' is essential for getting things done and feeling mentally energised.

Michael A Singer wrote in *The Untethered Soul*, 'If people were fed inside, feeling whole inside, you would not have a fraction of the problems outside. You would have much more harmony, much more togetherness'.

An energised head has a very similar feeling to an energised body. You feel capable and interested, stimulated and open to action. Your mind, like your body, has needs. It likes to feel in control. It needs 'useful beliefs'. It needs stimulation and understanding. It needs a plan. It needs some logic.

To improve your mental energy, you need to understand your mind. How does your mind work?

Are you a 'why' person? Do you need to know why something matters before you can care? If you are a 'why' person then your brain is constantly asking, 'Why? What does this matter? Why should I listen? Why should I care?'

My eldest son was like this. If I wanted him to do anything, I needed to help him understand why it was important, why I needed him to do it. Once I had him 'bought into the "why"', he was engaged and keen to go away and work out his own 'how'. 'Why' people often want to work things out for themselves once you have convinced them that something is useful or helpful.

I believe that all humans are on a sliding scale of most things. Neurodiversity is one of those things. 'Neurodiversity' is a word used to explain the unique ways in which people's brains work. While everyone's brain develops similarly, no two brains function exactly alike. Some people are very neurotypical, while others are super neurodivergent. I love that people are now beginning to understand that we all have different preferences and 'neuro needs'. Understanding our preferences and getting our needs met is essential for our mental energy.

I knew very early on that my brain did not work like other people's. I would observe others at school and ask constant questions: How did you work that out? Why do you think that? What can you see in your head when you are thinking about that? I was lucky to be a clever kid with healthy confidence, which meant that I made myself strong and not wrong. I noticed my preferences, the way my brain did things, and I used 'my way' as a strength. I refused to be made wrong by a teacher who did not understand me.

I am so grateful for my father's influence. He is a strong advocate for 'you do you' and taught me to challenge everything. He taught me about conviction and was incredibly supportive and encouraging. Children need advocates. Adults making children wrong makes me super angry! So many people I know were made wrong as kids. They were told they they were stupid and even made fun of for the way that their brains worked. It's a lot of work to 'make yourself right' as an adult, to tip yourself back up and unravel all the crap you have been told!

As a kid, I set out to give myself the things that I needed to function well. I would go and ask for more information about the things that did not make sense to me. I would trick people into drawing something for me if I couldn't understand it verbally. I have continued this as a parent. I am very big on fighting for what people need to function well. Do you need to be told or shown? Do you need to do something to understand it rather than just experiencing it theoretically?

It is well worth taking some time to learn about yourself, to understand what you need to be at your best. You already know, you just don't know that you know! There are many different learning styles, the main ones being visual, auditory, reading and kinesthetic. Podcasts are a wonderful example of how people can access information and learning in a way that suits them: being able to listen to things rather than having to read removes so many barriers for so many people.

I love visuals and images. My mind loves colour. I am a huge reader and have thousands of books. I organise my books by colour, in a rainbow and from the darkest to the lightest version of each colour. I think they look beautiful. Loads of people comment on how much time it must have taken to me to sort them and how gorgeous they look. They do look great, but more importantly, I am able to find any book very quickly because I often cannot remember the title or the author, but I can remember the colour of any book. And don't even get me started on the Dewey decimal system! Numbers in a list kill me. I was the messiest person to ever attend the Levin Public Library. I pulled all the books out and had them laid out all over the floor!

I could not read music as a kid. No matter how many people tried to teach me, my brain just turned off. I remember a piano teacher claiming, 'You are a clever girl – why can't you get this?' Finally, after years, my flute teacher Mr Mayclair said, 'Your brain is not getting this. Let's try playing by ear.' I could play anything anyone played for me, like a recording! I remember attending a school music event where loads of schools had come to gather. We were given a new piece of music, and Mr Mayclair sent another student and I outside to the back of the hall so she could play it for me before the event started!

The statement 'My brain needs…' is incredibly empowering. I have taught my kids never to be afraid to ask more questions, to say what they need. 'For me to understand this, I need to know…' The key to mental energy is to work out what you need and then go and get it! What are your mental preferences? What are the things that 'do your head in'? Do you need time to process information? Do you prefer in-person conversation or email or text messages? Do you need silence to think? Do you need other people to bounce off to create solutions, or do you need quiet space alone?

Gone are the days when we are all expected to be the same, to learn and absorb information in the same way. Children are no longer herded into classrooms, made to 'sit and concentrate' and made wrong for the things their brains do not cope well with.

Playing to our strengths is one of my favourite strategies. I spent three years running an international business school. We had an incredibly diverse team. The first thing I asked all the staff was what the thing was that 'did their head in' about their job. One person hated emails, so we used a message system. One person hated meetings, so she only came to every second meeting. One person needed lots of detail, so I would stay behind after meetings to make sure she got all the information she needed. Forcing people to do things that they are not good at or 'hate' is the fastest way to kill engagement and morale. Working in a way that works for people is a wonderful way to get the best out of them. It also brings awareness and connection to teams.

I always ask people how they would like information when I am sending it to them. Do they prefer voice messages? Do they like emails? Do they need time to absorb information, or are they reactive, intuitive responders? The greatest gift we can give any human is understanding. (That applies to ourselves as well!)

Giving people what they need is one of the most overlooked leadership strategies. Leadership is about getting the most out of people. Taking time to learn and provide the conditions for people to do well is vital to the success of any project, business or team.

Retaining amazing people is easy if they feel heard and understood. Happy people working in a way that works for them should be the goal of every employer.

## Your mind diet

Just like your body, your head requires an excellent diet to thrive. While we are conscious of what we put into our bodies, we are nowhere near as conscious of what goes into our heads. Negative people, violent TV shows, angry music, limiting environments, dramatic media – all of these things have a huge impact on how we feel, what we think and how we behave.

### Decide how you want your news served to you

I am not equipped to deal with the violence, trauma and disturbing stories that are shown on news shows. Reading news gives me the information without me having to deal with the drama. Be very choosy about the platforms you let into your life. You do not have to watch the news every day. Pick a time of day, pick a channel and pick a method for how you want to receive news.

## Be aware of your music diet

Music has the power to alter your mood and change your perceptions. Music can give you energy and motivation. It can soothe you, encourage you and inspire you. It can motivate you: during exercise, high-tempo music has been proven to improve people's ability to work out.

We connect with people using music, we share songs and playlists, and we follow and often idolise the people who produce or perform music.

It is no coincidence to me that rates of depression, anxiety and suicide have increased hugely in our young people when you look at the increase of negative themes in music over the past ten years. Lyrics are heavy, violent and angry. The types of words and vibrations being absorbed, coupled with the fact that people wear headphones for large parts of their days, means that people are marinating their brains in negative energy.

Think about the type of music you listen to and your normal mood or vibe. Sad and deep songs are not ideal to listen to every day if you are feeling low-vibe.

## You are what you read

Reading is one of my favourite pastimes. I love having the opportunity to disappear into someone else's head and learn something new. I adore self-help books and books about spirituality. Books have been my greatest teachers and have led me to amazing people and experiences.

I do not read novels. My brain cannot cope. I get very invested and worried about the characters. It's like they move into my head. When I'm trying to work, I find myself worrying about a character in a book and what will happen to them next. It's not that I don't like novels, I love them, but they distract me. Knowing this means that I can make a decision about allowing novels to be part of my world: they are not helpful to me when I am working on a big project or piece of work.

Knowing what your mind needs and responds to is important. I am thirsty for knowledge. I love learning about different perspectives. To be inspiring, I need to be inspired.

## Find your kind of people

I am allergic to negative people: people who complain and look for flaws all the time. I find them exhausting to be around. Limiting my contact with them is my best strategy, only making myself available in short bursts so that my energy isn't impacted.

In the previous chapter, I discussed contributors and contaminators – people who bolster or sap your energy. It's worth figuring out who these people are in your life so that you can maximise your time with the contributors and develop strategies to deal with the contaminators.

Who are the people you spend the most time with? Get out a pen and make a list. Some weeks we spend more time with people we work with than our own family.

Make sure that the people you surround yourself with serve you. Be intentional about who you hang out with. Be aware of the people who lift you up and weigh you down. I have friends who feel heavy and friends who feel light. I have people I can count on to go deep and people who will trivialise and bounce through any situation.

Contributors don't always have to be human: my pets contribute to my life because they make me feel happy. I have two beautiful cats who make me feel good just by being around. They don't do much, but I always enjoy being in their presence. Two years ago, we got a dog – or, rather, I should say I got my son a dog. I had planned to teach my son Felix about responsibility and discipline; instead, what we got was a whole lot of love. Max is just pure love. The saying 'get a dog and at least someone will be happy to see you when you come home' is so true! Max is delighted every time I arrive home. He is a joy. Not long after we got Max, Felix said to me, 'Mum, getting a dog is like buying a best friend.' I think he's right. Max is definitely a contributor.

## Belief

I spend a lot of my time speaking to people about their beliefs. When we hear the word 'belief', we often think of big things like believing in God or believing in yourself. While these big beliefs hold a lot of weight, I find it is the little beliefs that can really be the problem. They are often so small that we have no awareness of them, and yet they trip us up every day.

One of my most annoying habits is that I never hang up my clothes at the end of each day. I step out of them and into something else. The result of this behaviour is that I often have piles of clothes all over my bedroom, which is very messy and makes things hard to find. Eventually, I find that I have had enough, and I spend several hours tidying everything up while telling myself that this has got to stop as I do not have time to 'tidy my room' like a naughty teenager.

When I read James Clear's book *Atomic Habits*, I realised that the actual problem behind my messiness is that I do not believe I am a tidy person. I have always felt like a messy person. This was heavily affirmed for me as a child when I was constantly told that I was messy. After years of listening to this, I fully accepted this as a 'truth': that I am messy and, therefore, will always live in a shitty, messy room.

Except, beliefs can be changed. It is not easy, but it can definitely happen.

I used to believe that I was a late person. I was always late – in fact, I prided myself on it. I did not board a plane until my name was called and I never allowed travel time for any appointments. Years ago, my friend Fi called me at home and told me to put the television on, that there was something I should watch. I turned it on to catch Dr Phil saying to a guest on his show, 'So, you are always late. Even when you try to be early and you make an extra effort, you still arrive late'. He then asked the guest if she would like to know why she was always late, because he had an answer for her.

She said yes, and then they went to a commercial break! I was perched on the edge of the couch waiting for my diagnosis. Dr Phil returned and said that the reason she was always late was because she was arrogant. Arrogant! *How rude*, I thought. He really got my hackles up, and as I was about to turn off this rubbish he said, 'You think that nothing starts without you. You think that people will make allowances for you being late and that there is nothing wrong with keeping others waiting'. I was horrified. I had never seen myself as arrogant or self-serving, but something told me that Dr Phil was right and he was speaking this truth straight to me!

My friend was pleased. She had suffered my arrogance and tardy arrivals for far too long. I spent the next few days processing this and realised that I no longer wanted to behave that way. I also decided that being late was very unprofessional, and as a self-employed person I could not afford to tarnish my professional reputation with my consistent lateness.

So, I changed my belief. I decided that I was professional. I decided to honour others by never wasting their time or keeping them waiting. Changing my belief changed my lateness habit.

To determine whether a belief is a problem, I love to use Byron Katie's famous questions from her book *Loving What Love Is*:

- Is it true?
- Can you absolutely know that it's true?
- How do you react when you believe that thought?
- Who would you be without the thought?

So, is it true that I am a messy person? No. I am actually quite tidy, but when I am tired I cannot be bothered with the discipline of tidying as I go. When I say 'I am a messy person' – or, God forbid, someone else brings it up – I get angry. Intellectually, I have no interest in being a messy person. Who would I be without this thought? I would be a tidy person. I would be someone who respects her space (and the fact that my long-suffering husband cannot find his way to bed some nights!).

So, I changed my thought and the behaviour by asking myself a simple question: what would a tidy person do? A tidy person would put the coffee away after she uses it. A tidy person would hang up her clothes at night. A tidy person would put her cup into the dishwasher rather than stacking it on the bench.

You see, it is useful to me to believe that I am a tidy person. I love the idea of beliefs being useful. Chris Helder's *Useful Belief* is a wonderful wee book that gives a strategy outlook for whether or not your beliefs are useful.

My mum doesn't like Christmas. She never has. This started for her as a child, and as an adult and a mother Christmas was a chore. It meant loads of cooking, thinking about what to buy everyone for gifts and dragging out boxes of decorations. Every year, around October, she would start talking about how she was dreading Christmas, how she didn't like Christmas. Her belief that Christmas was awful was not useful. Christmas happens every year! It is bloody hard to ignore. So, she and I made a plan to help her feel better about Christmas. She took her power back, stopped doing all the stuff she thought she 'had to do' and removed the belief.

I meet Christmas grinches all the time. For whatever reason, Christmas is not their thing. But Christmas is not the problem: the problem is that that are wasting two months of the year bitching about it!

## Whatever you believe, you are right

If you believe that the world is full of arseholes, then you are right. If you believe that the world is a kind and glorious place, then you are right. And what you believe will be reflected right back at you.

I believe in angels. It's useful for me to believe that I have helpers available 24/7 who are only a whisper away.

My mum's sister was having a big operation. She was petrified: of hospitals, of anaesthetic, of the surgeon, the whole bit. I spoke to her a week before the planned surgery, and she was considering pulling out. She didn't think she could go through with it. 'You'll be fine,' I said with my ever-annoying positivity. 'How do you know!?' she asked. I told her that I had a group of special angels who were able to heal things and keep people safe. 'Oh yes,' she replied, thinking I was mad. I told her that I'd had a meeting with my angels and I had arranged for them to be at her surgery. I told her there would be eight of them standing around her bed in a circle. 'What will they do?' she asked. 'Just watch over you and make sure that everything goes well,' I said. She seemed happy with that.

The day of surgery came, and I spoke to her just before she went in. I told her that I had checked in with the angels and they were ready and waiting.

When she came to after the surgery, she was smiling. She said, 'Your angels were wonderful!' The surgeon said that everything went super well and he was very pleased. 'I told you they would look after you,' I replied.

When we left, my uncle walked us out to the carpark. As we walked down the stairs, I noticed a perfectly white feather sitting on the bottom step. I was so excited! I reached down to pick it up and handed it to my uncle. I told him to take it back up to my auntie to give her proof that the angels had been in the building!

I turned around, beaming, and my youngest daughter, Tilly, was staring at me. 'That feather probably came out of my puffer jacket,' she said! Tilly doesn't believe in angels – she believes in puffer jackets! I believe in angels. On that day, it was very useful for my auntie to believe in angels as well!

What is useful for you to believe? What beliefs do you currently have that are not useful?

I wrote in *Look Gorgeous, Be Happy*, 'Sometimes the only thing that you can change is your mind'. Changing our minds is one of the most powerful abilities we have as humans. Many of us have been told that it's not OK to change our mind. Many of us have been told that it's not OK to change, full stop – but that's another book!

The problem is that we attach our ideas to our identity. Then, when we change our minds, we think it changes who we are! I 'identify' as 'constantly curious', as a person with fluid thinking. This leaves me open to exploring ideas and new beliefs, and to being a lifelong learner. We don't know what we don't know. Why would we close ourselves off to potential new ways of thinking? Because we are committed to an identity! You will often hear people say things like, 'That's not what I do', 'I'm not that sort of person', or, 'That's not me'. Sometimes these statements come from self-awareness, from people who know who they are and what they are about, but sometimes they come from rigid self-identify and an inflexible mindset.

Getting your head to work for you is one of the best things you can do. You need to start with awareness. What are you like? Are you negative? Impulsive? Intense? Work out what you are like, and then you have two choices: own it or change it.

What you think, you become, and what you feel, you attract.

## We are addicted to problems

One of the biggest addictions that humans suffer from is an addiction to problems. People love problems. Some people are so deeply committed to being unhappy that they will constantly talk about their problems, smearing them all over everyone they meet, and when they are offered a solution, they will either reject it or quickly move onto to a newly discovered issue that they can make their next favourite problem.

The most interesting thing to me about problems is that they are never the problem. The problem is what you think about the problem! If you think something is bad or embarrassing or challenging, then you are right. Whatever you think, you are right.

There are two questions I like to ask myself when I encounter a problem: *What is really going on here?* and *How am I contributing to this problem?*

Asking myself *What's really going on here?* helps me to unpack the problem – the *real* problem. I think of problems like plants: the real problem is the not bit you can see – the leaves, the stalk – but is sitting under the ground in the roots.

Say your daughter keeps ignoring a curfew that you have given her. You are furious that she is not doing what you have said and listening to you. The stalk is that she is coming home much later than you would like. The leaves are the fact that you have wait up later and worry about her. But the root is that she is disrespecting you, that she is not respecting your rules, which, as her parent and leader of the family, you are entitled to make. The problem is not about lateness; it is about disrespect.

What's really going on here might be that you have been disrespected your whole life and feel that enough is enough. Every time your daughter is late, it reminds you of all the times that you have been ignored and disrespected in the past.

I like to take my plant unpacking one step further and ask myself, *How am I contributing to the problem? What am I tolerating, or how can I react differently so I am not contributing? Where am I disrespecting myself?*

Our mental commentary causes us the most problems. The narrative that we buy into creates so much suffering. If your mind is telling you that you are stupid, or that nothing ever works for you, or that you are not loveable or desirable, then that will cause you suffering.

Being aware of the story that is playing in your head and knowing that you have the power to change is a game changer for your mental energy. You are free to think whatever you want to think, but our conditioning makes us think otherwise. The beliefs that we have bought into create pain for us. As Marianne Williamson wrote in *A Return to Love*, 'It takes courage … to endure the sharp pains of self discovery rather than choose to take the dull pain of unconsciousness that would last the rest of our lives'.

How you spend your mornings, what you watch on your screens, who you share your life with and who has access to you will change your life. Give yourself permission to cancel a commitment, to decline a call, to change your mind, to be alone, to take the day off, to do nothing.

## Thinking in overdrive!

Overthinking is a huge energy waster. Using your head as a washing machine for things to go around and around is a waste of resources. The upside of overthinking is that it means you are clever! Dumb people cannot overthink – often they find thinking *once* a challenge.

I think of the thoughts in my head as goldfish in a bowl: they swim in one ear, do a lap and swim out the other. Sometimes they want to continually do laps! I notice them, acknowledge them and then tell them to leave. I started doing this as a meditation: sitting and focusing on my fish, seeing if I can get in charge of the goldfish in my head!

Meditation doesn't have to be the big deal that people think it is. I think of it as clearing your mind. I would have a meeting with each of the fish and ask them to go. I think they all want to be acknowledged; like most humans, the goldfish in my head want to be seen! But as the owner of my head, I want to be in charge of it. Imagine owning a building and seeing people come in whenever they want and stomp all over the place. Imagine if they stayed as long as they like. You would feel pissed off and powerless! These fish are squatters in your building! (I know I am mixing metaphors here – stay with me.)

You own your fishbowl, and it makes sense as a powerful person who wants to be in charge of their energy that you get to be in charge of these fish. After doing my fish meditation for a long time, I am now able to see a fish in my mind's eye as soon as it enters my head, acknowledge it, thank it and tell it to move on.

Fish arrive at odd times. Start noticing them. Start moving them. Don't be scared of your fish. If a fish turns up with a helpful thought, I find it best to look the fish in the eye. The thoughts in your head are incredibly powerful. They can ruin your life. If you have really scary or super intrusive big fish that won't leave, you really need to get some help. Get someone trained in thought-wrangling to sort them out.

Overthinking paralyses your mind and stops you from taking action. The root cause of overthinking is fear of getting things wrong. The antidote is action. Action keeps the darkness away and will get you out of your fear state. Mentally, as with physically, moving is the answer.

I think the secret to avoid being trapped in your head is to move into your body. Overthinking often comes from under-feeling. Under-feeling comes from fear, from being scared of your feelings (see Chapter 3!). Having spent years watching people being trapped in their heads and paralysed by overthinking, I am convinced that the way out of your head is through your body.

Physically getting your thoughts into your body can be fun. Visualise the thought in your head. What size is it? What shape is it? What music does it need? Dancing, drumming, stomping or shaking out your thoughts can be a wonderful experience.

A simple 'fuck off' shouted loudly will often move a thought away. Shouting is something we have been taught is not OK, especially women: we have been taught to be quiet and polite. Making a huge amount of noise will bring a lot of vibration to your body and shift some shit!

Roaring also works! I went to a roaring workshop with a wonderful teacher, Sylvia Rand. Sylvia spent two days teaching a room full of women to roar, to make deep, tonal sounds that came from the deepest parts of us – sounds that scared some of us, that were both empowering and scary. It's incredible the noises we can make! Finding somewhere where you can rant, stomp and act out your angst is a wonderful way of getting pesky thoughts out of your head.

## Procrastination paralysis

Any action will dissolve procrastination. Action is about getting stuff done, making shit happen. There's something that you could be doing right now to make your life better! What is it? Reading this book might be changing your life, but is there something you have been putting off? A phone call? A small job?

PUT THE BOOK DOWN AND GO DO IT!

Doing always makes you feel better afterwards! I am a big doer. Every day I think, *Right. What is one thing I can do today that's going to improve my life?* Talking, wishing and wanting will not get you the life you want. The world responds to action. Peace activist Thich Nhat Hanh said, 'My actions are my only true belongings. I cannot escape the consequences of my actions. My actions are the ground upon which I stand.'

Are you an actionator or a procrastinator? My beautiful friend Jacqui is a massive procrastinator. She is incredibly smart and also a chronic overthinker. She thinks about stuff all the time. She thinks deeply and from every side of everything! She has trouble taking action because she is constantly overwhelmed by possibility. We were talking one day and she said, 'You know how I think all the time and don't do stuff, and you just constantly do stuff? I think you are the opposite of a procrastinator – you are an actionator!'

Jacqui is right: I am an actionator. I'm really big on doing. I'm impulsive by nature and very impatient, so I tend to do things really quickly. Often, I don't think, I just do!

Don't get me wrong, I love to think. I can spend hours pondering and thinking and working through scenarios. But doing is everything.

If you're a procrastinator, the problem is that you're usually waiting for everything to be just right. So many of us get paralysed by inaction. My fix for this is a simple tool I call the 'bridge of action'. Take a piece of paper and draw a circle at each end. In the circle on the left, write today's date and describe where you are at with your current goal. In the circle on the right, write how things will be when you complete your goal. That is the easy part. The bridge is made up of the steps you need to take to get where you want to go. Between the circles, write down all the steps, no matter how small.

Before you go away on your holiday, or start your business, or renovate your house, what do you need to do? You might need advice; you might need to research. Put in place all the steps that will take you from where you are to where you want to be. This builds a bridge of action. Think of each step as a lily pad that will get you across the gap.

Action is tough if you haven't got a plan. I hear all the time: 'I'm hoping to do this or that'. Well, hope's not a bloody plan, is it? No, action is a plan. The bridge to action is your answer, so build a bridge and get over it. Get over yourself!

Planning your day, your week and your year will help you to live purposefully. Knowing your purpose helps you to stay on track, get things done and get in charge of your time. Planning everything allows you not to worry about anything. Work with what is rather than what if.

I cannot understand people who do not plan. I am with Benjamin Franklin when he said, 'Failing to plan is planning to fail'. All of us have been given a precious gift of time, and yet we are often so ineffective in the way we use it. Stuff that doesn't matter, people who are not important and tasks that we do not enjoy seem to gobble the bulk of it up. The thousands of people I speak to each year all nod their heads when I talk about doing too much of 'what we have to' instead of 'what we want to'. No wonder people are stressed out, burnt out and tapped out! Here's what you can do about it:

- Have regular meetings with yourself.
- Document what you have to do.
- Add in what you want to do.
- Block out time for your priorities – not other people's!

- Add in blocks of time for preparation and travel – getting places takes time.

Getting time and belief sorted are the keys to taking action. Allocating the right amount of time to the right things helps you to gain momentum. Believing in yourself and what you do propels you into doing. Getting shit done requires a level of belief and the time to achieve your goals.

Elizabeth Gilbert said, 'Perfectionism is just fear in fancy shoes and a mink coat.' When you're suffering from perfectionism and you're convinced that nothing will be good enough, you never actually do anything. You become paralysed by inaction. You worry, *What if it's not perfect? Maybe I can't send it; maybe I can't post it; maybe I can't ring them; maybe I can't apply for the job yet. You know, I'm waiting to be perfect, and then I'll apply for that job. I'm waiting to lose weight, and then I'll be happy. I'm waiting, waiting, waiting.* We're always waiting on something to be perfect. I don't think there's time to be perfect, there's just a time to be.

Action is often about doing things half-arsed. I often joke that because I have a big arse, doing stuff with only half of it is fine! Give yourself permission to half-arse something. What's the worst thing that can happen? What have you got to lose? 'Oh no, but if I don't rush in and do it properly, all hell will break loose.' I don't think so.

The truth is that most of the world won't notice! People are so self-absorbed, no one is really watching. I think it's more important just to get shit done. I know a woman who took three years to launch her business because she couldn't get her website just right. I told her, 'No one cares as much as you think they do'. Perfectionism's a bitch. What are you holding back from taking action on because you reckon you have to be perfect at it?

## Controlling your controllables

Being in control of my life has always been important to me. I like being the director of my movie. I love to be in charge. As self-esteem expert Jack Canfield said, 'You only have control over three things in your life: the thoughts you think, the images you visualise and the actions you take'.

Control has played a huge part in my life. As a reformed control freak, I feel fully qualified to talk about control and its many faces. I used to exhaust myself by literally trying to control everything: what my children wore, what my husband ate, what people around me did, what books my friends read! It was a crazy world. There is nothing wrong with knowing what you want in life, but micromanaging everything and everyone is no way to live well. I wanted to control the whole bloody world, and I completely exhausted myself in the process.

In his famous book *The 7 Habits of Highly Effective People*, Dr Stephen Covey included a famous model based on circles of concern, influence and control. The circle of concern includes things that you care about but have no control over, such as the weather or the economy. The circle of influence includes things that you cannot control but you can affect the outcome of to some degree, such as your health and relationships. The circle of control includes things you have complete control over, such as your thoughts and actions.

Many of us get these circles very muddled up! Trying to control things that are not in your circle of control is exhausting and a waste of your time. Controlling my energy and my actions are my two main focuses every single day.

Your circle of concern can include other people's beliefs, mistakes, actions and ideas. You don't have control over any of these things, so there is very little point in giving them your energy. Having children has taught me a lot about control: as your children grow and develop, they move out of your circle of control into your circle of influence, and then once they become adults they move further out into your circle of concern.

When I am feeling mentally overwhelmed, I draw two circles on a piece of paper. In the left, I write what I can control. In the right, I write what I cannot. I then rip the piece of paper in half and get on with doing the things on the left side – the things I *can* use my energy on.

In our busy worlds, we need to make decisions about our priorities and what we want to control. As someone obsessed with energy, here are the things I want to control (see figure 3 on page 115):

- **Response-ability.** We all have the power and ability to respond to life. When I am not in charge of my response, I am reactive. Being reactive wastes energy. It means that your body's adrenals are at the mercy of other people's behaviour!
- **Boundaries.** I get to decide what I will and won't do and what I will and won't tolerate. These are called the 'rules of me'! Check and update these regularly! You teach people how to treat you. Decide what is and isn't OK.
- **Nutrients.** I banged on about quality food in Chapter 1.
- **Mindset.** Managing the goldfish swimming in your head, getting to know your mind, making friends with it and getting in charge of it will change your life.
- **Mood.** Part of being an adult is taking responsibility for your behaviour. Your mood is part of that. Stomping around and being grumpy means that your energy is negatively impacting others.

- **Time.** You are on this planet for a limited number of days. Do not waste them. Use them for good. Make yourself happy. Make other people happy.
- **Belief.** Adjusting your beliefs will make your life easier. Personal growth comes from having the courage to re-examine what you believe often.
- **Effort.** Being enthusiastic is contagious. Making an effort is a decision. If something is worth your time, it is worth your effort.
- **Sleep.** Putting yourself to bed at a reasonable time is the smartest thing you can do. Good sleep equals good energy, which equals good living.
- **Money.** Money is energy. We all need to know how to understand it and get in charge of it. Money allows us to move energy around and through us. Having money removes friction: it means you can jump in and do things without waiting for another payday. Regardless of whether you have money or not, you can still be fucked up about it! Your beliefs, relationship and history with money all affect you. Many people carry a lot of shame around money. The way you interact with money will hugely impact the energy flow money has for you. My book *Everything YOU Want* has a chapter devoted to helping people get their money sorted.
- **Words.** Speaking your truth will save you time and energy. Say what you think. Mean what you say. Use your voice to express yourself.
- **Movement.** Find a way you like to move and do it often. Consciously move three times a day. Walk, stretch, dance, swim.

Figure 3: the things I want to control

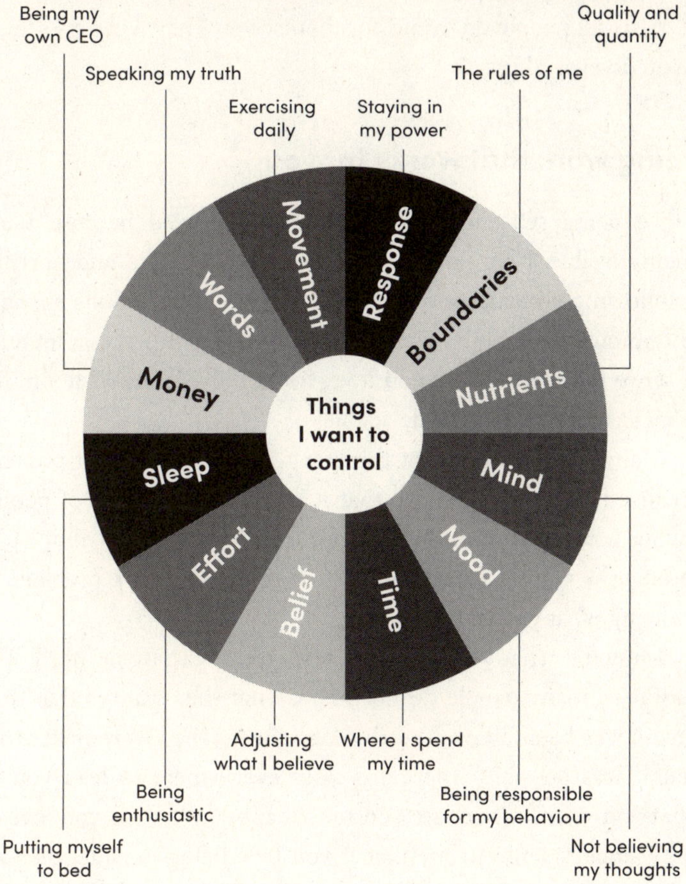


The combination of getting older and (I like to think) wiser made me realise that there is actually very little that we can control. Put your effort into the things that are within your control, and stop wasting your time worrying about things you are not in charge of. Pick your battles: go to war for the important stuff and let the little stuff go. Letting go of trying to control impossible stuff will free up so much time and energy.

Also, let people do things for themselves. They will never learn if you do everything.

## Doing work that works for you

I love being self-employed. I am self-employed because I am unemployable. I am not good at doing as I am told and horrible at following systems, and I get bored easily. Most adults spend a whopping 90,000 hours working in their lives. It makes a lot a lot of sense to do work that you love. As Kahlil Gibran wrote in *The Prophet*, 'Work is love made visible'.

Many people think that this is not possible. It is not possible because they do not believe that it is. I am a huge fan of people having what they want. In my book *Everything YOU Want*, I talk about how getting what you want is not as big of a problem as knowing what you want.

Knowing what you want will lead you to what you need. The reason so many people do not know what they want is that they have never been allowed to think about it. They were never told that it was possible. There are clues everywhere to lead you to what you want. Where are you most happy? What do you love to do? It makes sense to me that if you love being outside, then an outdoor job would fill your boots. If you are drawn to children, then teaching them would be a delight.

Many of us were raised in a time when we didn't have a lot of choice about what we did. Now, the possibilities are endless. However, change takes courage. Change is uncomfortable. Sometimes change is less profitable. Money is not the only currency we get from work. The money is not worth it if you get no energy from it. As the famous saying goes, 'Find a job you love and you will never have to work a day in your life again'.

I once spoke at a large company conference about energy: about where it comes from and why it is so important. A month later I sent the CEO an email about another workshop we had discussed. Her assistant replied saying that she was no longer with the company. I sent her a private message to wish her well with what was next and to check that she was OK. She replied saying she had been meaning to reach out as her quitting was all my fault! She'd had an epiphany while I was talking that she was not enjoying her role, that a job that had once excited her was now very draining. She quit the following week. She had no idea what she was going to do, but she knew that she had to do something, because her fatigue in her role was not allowing her to be the wife, mother and friend she wanted to be. She said, 'I was grumpy all the time. Life is too short!'

## The exhausted provider

You might know one. You might be one. Exhausted providers are capable, good at what they do. They are able to solve problems and sort shit out – they constantly come up with solutions. They are committed. They do what they say they are going to. They don't like letting people down. They are wonderful parents, workers, bosses and friends. They care. They are kind and serve to others. They want their people to be happy. They often give at the expense of themselves.

The world offered us a big promise: that if we were 'good', if we did all the right things, then we would be rewarded. We would be happy.

Exhausted providers work their arses off. They pride themselves on being 'good': good daughters or sons, good parents, good friends, good bosses, good team members. They live off the promise that if they play by the rules, do the right thing and tick all the boxes, they will be content and get 'the life they deserve'. But usually, they just feel more and more pressure. They are fried. They are disillusioned. They can't even tell people that they are unhappy because outwardly everything looks great!

Exhausted providers live on a raft of responsibility. They are responsible for everyone from a very early age – for looking after brothers and sisters, for fulfilling the dreams of their parents, for everyone and everything – or so they think!

I see this all the time with the amazing people I meet and mentor. People come to my events with all the trappings of success, but they have lost the light in their eyes. Stage one: they are a robot going through the motions. Stage two: they are super fragile and one hug away from falling apart. They have trapped themselves in a mouse wheel and are doing their best to look happy about it! They are trying to keep calm and carry on, convinced that if they do enough it will come right.

I have been there! As a recovering people-pleaser, rescuer and control freak, I get it! I wrote a poem that describes how I felt.

***The Exhausted Provider***

*I'll sort it!*
*I've got this*
*It's fine*
*I say*
*I'm calm*
*And consistent,*

*It feels heavy*
*Some days.*
*Expectations and*
*Obligations*
*I'm happy*
*To pay.*
*Responsibility's*
*My thing*
*In the sun*
*I make hay*
*I go get a coffee*
*To boost my energy*
*People laughing and*
*Socialising in the cafe.*
*Could someone*
*Acknowledge*
*My duty and hard work?*
*Obligation has become*
*My way.*
*The pressure is huge,*
*Mustn't let it show*
*'Effortless effort'*
*A day off if I may?*
*I'm there for everyone*
*Except myself*
*Smiling on the outside*
*I want to run away.*

All 'should's are based on our conditioning. As you start to notice it, it will get more and more obvious!

We need to get more present to the energies that give us 'should's – the people, the places, the roles. Only when we are aware can we find the total freedom, adventure and joy we are looking for. As we let go of 'should' and make space to ask, 'What do I want?' a higher, truer life can unfold:

- **Get honest.** How do you feel? Angry? Sad? Disillusioned? Write down or voice out loud how you are really feeling. This can be hard after so many years of performing and pretending.
- **Don't make any sudden movements.** Don't make any decisions. Breathe and take some time to consider. Consider everything!
- **Create some space.** A weekend away? A holiday? Find a way to get away. Take yourself to a place where no one needs you. It might be another city; it might be a tiny house in the country.
- **Reconnect.** Do something you used to do. Go somewhere you used to love. Talk to someone who knew your old self.
- **Decide.** What do you want? What is working? What is not?
- **Get a plan.** You might need help to do this. An accountability buddy or a mentor can help you, guide you and hold you to your plan.

You also need to communicate. Communication is the single greatest tool that we have, and yet so many people fail to use it. We live in a self-obsessed world where we assume that everyone knows what is happening in our lives and can read our minds, and then we are constantly disappointed when they fail to support us.

Tell the people around you what you need from them and stop the guesswork:

- Tell your family what you have on at work and warn them of high-stress times.
- Tell your colleagues if you are under pressure at home so they can offer you support or space.
- Ask others what you can do for them to help their workload.

Emily Dickinson wrote, 'I dwell in possibility'. I want to spend less of my life dwelling in obligation and more 'dwelling in possibility'. It feels much heavier to say that I 'should' lose weight, go to the gym, spend less money, spend more time with relatives and recycle all my rubbish than that I 'can' do all these things!

*

Turn the page to find ideas and suggestions to Get, Guard and Give mental energy.

# Getting mental energy is all about intentions!

Your intentions are what will give you mental energy. The work you put into being intentional makes all the difference to your mental clarity. Proactive intention means planning, communication and controlling what you can. We waste so much mental energy when we are not purposeful, when we don't communicate with those around us and when we waste our mental energy trying to control things that we cannot.

- **Embrace the power of changing your mind and identity:** Recognise that changing your mind and evolving your identity is a powerful ability. Often, people resist change because they associate it with a shift in their core identity. By acknowledging that it's OK to change, you open yourself up to new ideas, lifelong learning and the exploration of different beliefs. Avoid rigid self-identity as it can lead to inflexibility.
- **Unpack problems to identify the root issues:** Problems are often not what they appear to be on the surface. Like plants, they have roots hidden beneath. When facing an issue, dig deeper to find the underlying causes. This helps you address the real problem rather than just its symptoms.
- **Challenge and change the narrative in your mind:** Your inner narrative greatly influences your perception of reality. Challenge negative or limiting beliefs that hinder your personal growth. Be aware that the way you think about a problem determines your experience of it.

- **Move from overthinking to taking action:** Overthinking can be draining and lead to paralysis. To overcome this, shift from overthinking to taking action. Action not only resolves issues but also provides momentum and clarity.
- **Physically engage with your thoughts to release them:** Visualise your thoughts as goldfish swimming in a bowl. Acknowledge them, then gently release them. This process helps you gain control over your mental space.

## Guarding mental energy is all about being gentle with ourselves!

We need to learn to be gentle with ourselves. You can only do the best you can in any given moment, which will be different on different days. You deserve all the love and kindness that you so readily give to others. Cut yourself some slack. Give yourself some space. Give yourself permission to do nothing. Every once in a while, put a line through three things that can wait and take the day off: take yourself to the movies or binge-watch some terrible TV.

Ask for help! When you ask other people to help you, you give them an opportunity to give, to be generous and to demonstrate their love and appreciation for you. Doing everything yourself is unhelpfully independent. 'I really need your help' is an incredibly vulnerable and powerful thing to say.

Pausing is gentle. It gives you time to consider. Our world is so fast that we can forget we have the ability to pause! When's someone asks you to do something – it might be a favourite person offering you an opportunity – the best response is to pause, to give yourself minute and allow your body time to take the request from your ears and let it travel through your mind, then down through your heart and finally to your gut. Listen to the messages you receive from each place, then let the request travel back to your throat where you can voice a response. No one needs an instant response. My favourite strategy is if it is not a 'HELL YES' then I sleep on it. You are allowed space to consider.

- **Practise self-compassion:** Recognise that you're human and that it's OK to have limitations. Be kind to yourself, especially during challenging times. Give yourself permission to rest and recharge. Taking days off occasionally and doing nothing can be essential for mental rejuvenation. Remove any guilt associated with self-care.
- **Ask for help:** Allow others to support you. You don't have to carry the weight of the world on your shoulders. Asking for help allows others to lend their support and demonstrates vulnerability, fostering deeper connections.
- **Pause:** Take your time to respond to requests or decisions. Avoid reacting hastily; instead, take a moment to consider the implications and respond thoughtfully. This practice helps you make more considered choices.

## Giving mental energy is all about consideration!

Consideration is a beautiful thing. People with great mental energy are able to be considerate. They are able to think things through, to be thoughtful.

Shoe-shifting means thinking about things from another person's perspective. Next time you are with someone, try moving into their shoes. Think about how they are seeing the discussion you are having. Great leaders are able to consider the concerns of others before they are told about them. They are able to consider the potential outcomes not just for themselves but for others.

- **Plan your days, weeks and years intentionally:** Planning is a powerful tool for managing your mental energy. Getting all your plans out of your head and onto paper or a device clears up space in your brain. It also allows you to be intentional about how you structure your time, aligning it with your goals and priorities.
- **Communicate your needs and boundaries effectively:** Effective communication is key to giving and receiving energy. Clearly express your needs and boundaries to others, reducing misunderstandings and conflicts.
- **Focus on what you can control and let go of the rest:** Recognise that you can't control everything. Concentrating your energy on what you can control will help you to let go of factors beyond your influence. This mindset reduces stress and increases efficiency and capacity. When you are clear about what's in your circle of control, you have more energy to direct into those things.

# 5

# SPIRITUAL ENERGY

*'We are not human beings having a spiritual experience. We are spiritual beings having a human experience'.*

~ Pierre Teilhard de Chardin

Before we can begin talking about spiritual energy, I need to say that your spiritual energy depends on what you believe. What you believe has a big impact on what you experience in life! I am a huge fan of people choosing their beliefs. I am fascinated by what people believe and spend a lot of time helping people track down where their beliefs come from.

My husband was born into a Catholic family, and when our first child was born the subject of our son being raised Catholic came up. I politely told my father-in-law that I had no interest in 'giving' Oscar a set of religious beliefs. To me it felt the same as deciding on the career that this tiny little baby should have: it was not my decision. Spirituality is unique to every individual, and it is your right to define and find your spirituality as you see fit. It is your own personal journey in which you connect to yourself and the divine. I remember saying that if Oscar grew up and wanted to become Catholic, I would fly him to Rome and take him to the Vatican – but it would be Oscar's choice.

Years later, my youngest son Felix asked me to buy him a 'church shirt'. I asked him what he meant and he said, 'You know, something smart to wear to church'. He had picked this up from a church-run kindergarten that he was attending. We bought him a very smart button-down collared shirt and he became a Baptist for about three weeks.

My mother is not religious but was a well-trained Presbyterian. My father is an atheist. As a child I was taken to Sunday school; I coloured in drawings of Jesus and Mary, which my father would scoff at when I brought them home. I am so grateful for this contrast. I got to fit in among these two people's beliefs and decide where I sat, like living in a real-life sliding scale.

I loved churches – the ritual and ceremony and beautiful windows and ornate furniture – and always wanted to be part of the grandness of religion. However, while my body felt comfortable in this beautiful environment, my head was constantly questioning everything that was being said! *How do you know Jesus said that? Why would someone do such a thing?* My father's influence encouraged me to question everything. I have never enjoyed rules or being told what to do. I have zero interest in having my beliefs limited or wronged. My basic life philosophy is that we are here to experience, to love and to enjoy our lives.

From an early age, I became a 'spiritual freelancer'. I took things that made sense to me and started constructing my own belief system.

## Spirituality

Spirituality is a big topic. I think of spirituality as an individual practice based on peace and purpose, in comparison to religion, which is a specific set of organised beliefs and practices usually shared by a community or group.

Stepping into my spirituality has helped me to cultivate a connection with my soul, to meet my higher self. It has helped me get to know who I was before I was told who to be! It helps me to feel safe, supported, guided and surrounded by a team of supporters and advisors. My spiritual energy allows me to access my light. It allows me to live lighter.

There is a lot of fear around even the word 'spiritual'. This mostly comes from religions that tell us anyone operating outside of the rules is bad, evil or dangerous. It makes perfect sense: if I were running a fear-based organisation and wanted masses of people to believe the same thing, I would be cautioning people away from free thinking and agency!

I have met a lot of people who have decided to bow out of the spiritual–religious conversation completely. They do this by pretending that they are atheists. Atheists are people who do not believe in God or in a higher power or spiritual force of any kind. It is easier to bow out of the conversation than it is to take the time to discover and unpack your beliefs. I think atheists lack imagination – there are so many things you could believe.

If you are unsure, I urge you to read on, to notice your reactions. When are you thinking, *This sounds like a bunch of bullshit*? When are you thinking, *Shit, that feels quite comforting*? My goal is not to convert you into a spiritual person by the end of this chapter. My goal is for you to understand spiritual energy and all its benefits.

There are many definitions of the word 'spiritual':

> 'Being concerned with the human spirit or soul as opposed to material or physical things'
>
> 'A sense of connection to something higher than ourselves'
>
> 'The recognition of a feeling or sense or belief that there is something greater than myself, something more to being human than sensory experience, and that the greater whole of which we are part is cosmic or divine in nature'.

I like Brené Brown's definition from her second book, *The Gifts of Imperfection*:

> 'Spirituality is recognising and celebrating that we are all inextricably connected to each other by a power greater than all of us, and that our connection to that power and to one another is grounded in love and compassion. Practicing

spirituality brings a sense of perspective, meaning, and purpose to our lives.'

When I start talking about spirituality, I often come up against some myths and odd ideas that people want clarity on:

- **You do not need a guru.** I love the saying that when the student is ready, the teacher will appear. This may not be an actual person – it might be a book, a course or a workshop. My advice is to become your own guru. Take a teaspoon of all the ideas offered to you.
- **There is no race to win or levels you need to achieve!** There is no finish line to cross. One mountain will lead you to another; one book will open you up to another. Spirituality is a relationship between you and the universe that you live. It is a continuous process of evolution and growth.
- **You do not have to act, talk and live in a certain way to be spiritual.** You're born spiritual! Divinity is your true nature. When people start exploring spirituality, they are awakening their essence, reconnecting to themselves. This does not require you to wear bells around your ankle, dress in tie-dyed fabrics and chant all day.
- **Being spiritual doesn't not mean you are always positive!** Being in a constant state of gratitude and positively is not the goal. Being connected to yourself and making peace with people and situations is one of the benefits. Constant pretending is toxic. You are still a person having a human experience.
- **You can be spiritual and religious at the same time.** The truth is, you can be whatever you want! Your spiritual essence is a personal path that may or may not include an organised

> community with scriptures and a church. Your soul doesn't differentiate between spirituality and religion! Some of the most inspiring spiritual teachers I know work with bibles, angels, crystals, prayers, tantra – all of the things.

Spirituality and religion are often opposed to one another. There are core differences between the two – rules and definitions that set them apart. Religion has rules in the form of rituals rooted in dogma and ideology. Spirituality has no rules except for one, which is to follow your heart.

Some religions have a restricted definition of God that leaves no room for discussion. Spirituality doesn't restrict how you refer to or perceive higher powers – you define them as per your unique experience. When my children were little, we used to teach them about inside voices and outside voices. I think about this when I discuss beliefs with people. Some have an inside God and others have an outside God! Whether your version of God is inside or outside, being yourself with 'God' is the goal.

When my eldest daughter was eight years old, she went to a friend's house for a sleepover. She packed up her little bag and took her own pillow. At 8 p.m. that night I received a phone call from the mother of my daughter's friend. She was very concerned as Ruby had a 'small bag of rocks' in her pillowcase. The woman told me that they were a Christian family and did not believe in crystals. She asked me to come and pick up the offending crystals as she did not allow any form of witchcraft in her house. I said I would pick up Ruby as I did not want her in their house!

On the drive home, Ruby summed it up perfectly when she said, 'It's weird that they don't like rocks, Mum – didn't God make the rocks!?'

## What is spiritual energy?

Spiritual energy fuels your purpose, self-esteem and intuition.

Whether you identify as a spiritual person or not, you are a soul on a mission. You are here to learn, experience and grow through some lessons. In my world view, your soul has many missions. It lives many lives. Each life is loaded with opportunities to grown and learn. Your soul picks a body, a family and the circumstances that it needs to learn what it needs or wants to learn.

I love the idea that we choose our lives. I believe that each of us has a soul contract, that our soul chooses our families, our bodies, our lessons, and how and when it will die. It has a plan. Believing this helps me to trust, to relax and surrender to the fact that I do not need to know everything because there is a divine plan. It also helps me to be more accepting. Believing that 'no soul dies without its permission' has helped me to be incredibly comfortable with death.

Even when death seems tragic, I am comforted by the fact that there is a bigger lesson at play. There is always a plan. The shitty bit is that we do not know what the plan is. That is the wrestle of being human – of trying to make sense of things that don't.

I was working with a woman last year and we were talking about children. I made a comment that 'our children choose us', and she got very annoyed! 'I hate that theory!' she said. 'It makes me so angry when people say shit like that! It makes no sense. Why would a child choose terrible parents, dysfunctional people and potentially a shitty life?'

'Because that's what the child's soul needed to learn', I replied.

(I went on to say, 'in my world view'. I always start with that, because this is my world view. I do not expect anyone to agree with or take on my beliefs. I hope that they might help and offer a different way of thinking for someone, but I am a huge fan of the power of freedom and believe that everyone has the ability to choose their beliefs.)

So, 'In my world view,' I continued, 'we are all souls who get the magnificent opportunity to take a trip to "life school" – a place where we get to experience a human body. Living in a body that allows us to experience emotions and feelings and, ultimately, to learn. At the end of our life, we return to the spirit world, do a reconciliation, and then choose another mission and return to learn that.'

## Life school

How lucky are we? We won a lucky ticket to, as poet Mary Oliver wrote in her poem 'The Summer Day', 'one wild and precious life'! I have always thought that being alive is a gift. It's a gift that I do not think enough of us are grateful enough for. I want people to spend more time in awe of their lives, of the wonder of creation and all of the magic that comes with living in a body and experiencing this world.

I like to start my day with feeling 'lucky': lucky I woke up (thousands don't); lucky I can step out of my bed (thousands can't); lucky I am loved (thousands aren't) and live in a beautiful house surrounded by everything I could ever need (thousands don't). Whenever I am feeling stressed or out of control, I try and force myself to go into 'lucky' mode. Contrast that with the reality that being a human is hard! Really hard, sometimes. Life school is where we get to come and learn.

I love the idea that everything happens *for* us, not *to* us. It's a small distinction that changes everything. If you believed everything that happened to you was in some way part of a large plan – a plan created for the greater good of your soul's growth – life might become a completely different ballpark!

My youngest daughter was seven years old when she was diagnosed with type 1 diabetes. It was a huge shock; I knew nothing about type 1 and what it meant. We suddenly had a child whose pancreas couldn't produce enough insulin for her to survive on and who we needed to learn how to keep alive. The enormity of the situation began to sink in: this was permanent; this was big. There is no magical formula to solve all your problems when you have a child with type 1 diabetes, and it actually never gets easier. Every day is different depending on the level of activity, the food eaten, their mood and hormones – the regime changes. And it never stops. Never. Not for Christmas, Not for birthdays, not even so you can sleep through the night.

On day two we were feeling bit sorry for ourselves. I went and got us coffee from the hospital cafe. I picked up the newspaper and read that a little boy had been swept off a beach by a rogue wave while walking with family on the shore. He was gone.

I walked back up to our hospital room and announced how lucky we were! We were on the wrong side of a lot of new things. We had a lot to learn. We had to stick needles into our little girl multiple times a day for the rest of her life – but at least we had her. We were the lucky ones.

Believing that I am lucky and always supported by the universe helps me immensely. It has gotten me through some tough times.

Over six years, three of my children were diagnosed with type 1 diabetes. The week of the third diagnosis, my friend turned up to the hospital with a card saying, 'God only sends you what you can handle,' I nearly threw it at her. Then I opened it, and on the inside it said, 'He must have on file that you are a fucking ninja'! I laughed and laughed! I was a ninja, and a lucky ninja at that!

I could not do what I do or handle what I handle without my spiritual belief system. These are my five most powerful personal beliefs:

1. Everything happens *for* me.
2. I will always be OK.
3. I am guided.
4. I can do what I want.
5. I am an endless source of energy and love.

Believing these things has changed my life.

### 1. Everything happens *for* me

While it often doesn't feel like it at the time, things always happen for the best. I have been angry in the past when I didn't get something I thought I wanted – it didn't appear to want me! There have been very few things in my life that I really, truly wanted that I didn't get. Not getting these things caused me a lot of pain, humiliation and angst. Looking back now, I know that they were not meant for me. They were things my ego and personality wanted, but not my soul. They were not for my greater good. There were signposts everywhere – I overlooked them all. I arrogantly stomped onwards, convincing myself I was right without reading the signs or listening to my intuition, my 'inner ding' (as Louise Hay calls it).

Not getting things can be the biggest blessing. There is a gift hidden inside every disaster. Usually, it is very hard to find, and sometimes it is not discovered until years afterward.

### 2. I will always be OK

The belief that I will always be OK gives me a huge amount of energy. It saves me wasting time worrying. It stops me falling into fear. Feeling protected and supported is wonderful. My favourite definition of confidence is not that I will always know what to do; it is that even when I don't know what to do, I will be OK.

Humans are amazing. Think of all the times you thought you were not going to be OK, and yet here you are. I love the statistic that we have all survived 100% of the worst things that have happened to us. This gives me great confidence that we will continue to be OK! Despite all the times when you thought, *I will never survive if X happens to me*, here you are surviving!

I trust myself and my guides to guide me.

### 3. I am guided

Listen to your higher self. How many times have you overridden a feeling you have had and regretted it? This often happens when we make a decision in haste without 'checking in'. Your higher self has your back! It is sending you messages all the time. Your higher self is your intuition, which is often supported by messages from your guides. I believe we all have guides that are assigned to us at birth, and they are always guiding us – that's what our 'guides' do. They guide! Believing that you have a trusty team of support angels and guides available is incredibly comforting. Take time to listen to them! Take time to pause.

Your higher self will give you warnings about things that are not right for you, but it will also nudge you towards things that are perfect. Notice things that light you up, things that make you feel something. Don't question them. Notice what your eyes are drawn to, what things intrigue you. They are all clues to your soul's longing. As the novelist Stendhal put it, 'I note the echo that each thing produces as it strikes my soul'.

## 4. I can do what I want

Even though I believe that I have a soul contract, I still believe that I have free will. Our soul contract is designed for our highest good – it's an ideal plan for what our soul wants and needs to learn or experience. However, all of us have 'sliding door' moments when we choose one thing or another that alters our life course. This is the personal power of every human being: while we might have a 'destiny' or a master plan, we can do what we want. Believing that I can do what I want gives me an enormous amount of energy. It empowers me. It gives me space and ease. Next time you are feeling restricted or 'hemmed in', try repeating to yourself, 'I can do what I want'. You will feel freer and more energised.

## 5. I am an endless source of energy and love

Believing that I am a regenerating source of love and energy increases my energy. It also makes me more loving. I remember when I was overdue with my third baby. My eldest son asked me if I would still love him as much when the baby came. I explained to him that when my tummy grew a baby, my heart grew a new compartment filled with more love. I made it up on the spot, but it felt right! Love is a verb; it is a doing word. The more we love, the more we love. There is no limit to the number of people that I can love, no end to the energy I can give – but only if I care for myself and create the conditions for energy and love in my world. I need to have energy and love to give energy and love. You cannot give what you do not have.

✦

Take this time to examine your own beliefs. Maybe you want to borrow some of mine? Unpacking your spiritual beliefs is the beginning of tapping into your spiritual energy.

## Your soul

Each of our souls is encoded with a 'soul vibration', which is designed for the impact we were created to make. Your vibration is your responsibility – it is up to you to manage it. When your spiritual energy is good, it increases your vibration. The things that light up your soul expand your universal energy field.

Your soul has memories of your previous lives and experiences. It is able to be present in your current self while preparing you for the future. It has a completely different perspective from your 'human self'. Your soul always has wisdom and guidance. It is a source of solutions. Spending time connecting to your 'soul self' gives you access to your divine intelligence, which can dramatically improve your life, replacing worry with trust and faith.

Believing that you have a 'soul self' is a huge step. I explain it like this:

- You have a body, which contains organs and a personality. This is your 'self'.
- You have a 'soul'. This is your spiritual essence.
- The universal energy field connects to and communicates with your soul. In the universal energy field, there is no separation. No one is better than anyone else; nothing is more or less valuable.
- Your soul and self are contained in a vibrating bubble called an 'aura'. Your aura is a holding pen. It holds onto all kinds

of energy and experience that your body is unaware of.

Your aura expands and contracts based on your vibration.

I love the concept of universal energy. I think of it as an ocean of glitter. In the ocean of glitter, we are all tiny little specks. You are also the whole universe! Being part of a larger, collective vibration removes the feeling of separation from others. It helps us to be aware of the collective energy that we are always living in and contributing to.

I once went to a workshop held by the wonderful Neale Donald Walsch. Neale is a spiritual teacher and wrote the bestselling book *Conversations with God*, another that changed my life. (See the back of this book for a recommended reading list.) The night I went to see Neale, he opened the event by saying to a crowd of 500 people, 'You are the only one in the room'. Confused, I looked at my friends, who were clearly in the room, and they looked back at me. Neale went on to suggest, 'What if everyone in the room is a reflection of you?' I was confused at first and then immediately fascinated. I thought *I'll play your silly game, Neale!* What if that was true?

I looked around the room. There was a woman in front of me who had been rustling a plastic bag for the whole first ten minutes of the show. She was annoying. I then thought about the fact that I am often annoying. Maybe Neale was right. Maybe she was me! Maybe I was her!

That comment changed my life. I cannot meet other people now without considering that they are a reflection or part of me. It's the most wonderful way to move away from separation, to stop comparing humans with each other. It moves me closer to the concept that we are all one.

As a soul who has had hundreds or possibly thousands of lives, or 'experiences', you will have some scars. Your soul will have been battered and bruised and will have some memories and trauma from its travels. I call these 'soul scars'. The reason I bring them up is because they will be a drain on your energy. These scars are constantly there. Like a browser open on your energy's desktop, they are using up energy.

Imagine that you have a soul scar of rejection. Your soul has a memory of being rejected, and so, for some weird reason unbeknown to you (as a human body with a personality), you are constantly worried about being rejected: you might be anxious that your partner is not as invested in your relationship as you are, or you might be needy and demanding with your friend group. It seems odd and irrational because you don't have any life experience of being rejected. This is how your soul scar is showing up.

Table 2 shows various soul scars and their corresponding solutions and soul desires.

Table 2: soul scars and desires

| Soul scar | Solution | Soul desire |
|---|---|---|
| Humiliation | Self-respect | Elevation |
| Rejection | Self-acceptance | Approval |
| Betrayal | Self-loyalty | Faithfulness |
| Abandonment | Self-love | Connection |
| Injustice | Self-forgiveness | Neutrality |

The bad news is that most of us have many of these – often all of them!

Respect, acceptance, loyalty, love and forgiveness, which many of us are taught and honour when it comes to other people, are completely different stories when it comes to ourselves. The work of learning to like yourself is huge. Self-respect, self-acceptance, self-loyalty, self-love and self-forgiveness are all big work, and very few humans can be bothered healing. It is way easier to disregard these scars, but they don't go away. They are in your soul, and your soul is eternal!

These scars constantly leak your energy. They drain your aura. Here is how they do this and what you can do about it:

- If you have a scar of **humiliation**, you will lack confidence and try to control everything, and will procrastinate to the point of missing valuable opportunities. Focus on self-confidence and trust. Be confident that you will be OK.
- A scar of **rejection** will exhaust you as you constantly seek approval and try to keep up with everyone around you, believing that you will never be good enough. No one can reject you if you accept yourself as you are.
- If you have the scar of having suffered from **betrayal**, you will lack boundaries and be constantly people-pleasing so that you are kept around. You will put everyone ahead of yourself, never having enough energy or time for yourself. Be gentle to and generous with yourself. Know your non-negotiables so you do not betray yourself.
- **Abandonment** scars show up as a lack of self-love and self-care. You need to remember who you are, connect with yourself, appreciate yourself and show yourself loving care. Take great care for your own well-being and happiness.

- If you have an **injustice** scar, you carry a backpack of shame and/or anger. You have trouble with self-forgiveness. You cannot imagine being neutral on anything as you are deeply angry. You need to learn to be accepting so you can move forward.

## Auras

I believe that your aura is an electromagnetic field that radiates from you, like a large egg that stretches up above your head and down into the ground below your feet. Most auras extend about an arm's length from your physical body. Your aura is an extension of your being. I think of my aura as my spiritual skin, like living with a huge water balloon around me! I often get the giggles when I am out and I can see everyone in their energy bubbles bouncing into each other. When your aura is strong, it protects you. You feel robust. When your aura is weak, you feel vulnerable.

This works globally as well as personally. Our auras combine to create the current 'collective consciousness'. The energy of the world rises and falls based on all of our combined energy fields. You can literally feel when a country is hurting: when a huge disaster happens or when a war breaks out. The energy of the people affected affects all of us.

The quality of your aura is the result of your thoughts (mental energy), feelings (emotional energy) and actions (physical energy). People who are negative and unkind will have a heavy, dark aura. When you first meet someone and you get a 'vibe', and you say things like, 'He's got weird energy', or, 'She feels heavy', it is their aura that you're picking up on. There is literally a vibration that you are responding to.

## Your energy centres

Your auric field is made up of energy from your chakras. We have over 100 energy centres in our bodies, but seven main ones, which are called chakras:

1. Root or base chakra
2. Sacral chakra
3. Solar plexus chakra
4. Heart chakra
5. Throat chakra
6. Brow chakra
7. Crown chakra

The word 'chakra' comes from the Sanskrit word for 'wheel'. Chakras can best be described as the spinning vortexes of energy located vertically along the spine. The seven chakras in your physical body appear like disks of light. They transport information and energy to over 70,000 meridians, sharing energy along lines that run through the body like a river system.

We are taught a lot about our physical body, about our organs and other human anatomy, but we know little about our energy body. Our energy body communicates with our physical body, transmitting information. Our energy body knows everything! It holds all of our secrets: how we feel about ourselves, how we feel about our world, what we are afraid of, what we feel bad about.

I think of chakras as secret cupboards inside us. Each of our chakras relates to different organs and glands and can have a huge impact on our physical and emotional well-being. The can be open or blocked, overactive or underactive. When we are born, they are open and beautiful; life experience and our beliefs block them.

Getting to know your chakras is a great way to understand your energy. Get to know yourself: open up these secret cupboards stored with energetic information!

This book's appendix shows themes, areas of concern, remedies and support for each of the chakras. You can have your chakras balanced by an energy healer: they might use pendulums, muscle testing or their hands to read each centre.

## Taking time to connect

We must detach from our outer world to access our inner world. Being still and creating some space is the secret to connecting with your higher self. It doesn't have to be a ceremony; it doesn't require the help of any professionals. Just sit down, shut up and stop for a moment.

Taking time to connect feels weird at first. Often, nothing happens. You sit down and wait for something magical to happen, and all that actually happens is that you remember you have not fed your cat! However, over time it will get better. Sit and smile. Making time to do this every day is a wonderful practice.

I like to sit and visualise my chakras. I start at the base of my spine. I visualise a red circle. I see if it is spinning. I see if it feels bright or dark. I check in with my energy and how it feels. I then move up my body, working the relevant colour and area of the body. By the time I have reached my crown, I feel very relaxed and connected.

This is my DSP: my daily spiritual practice. Your DSP can be anything: it could be surfing; it could be journalling. I like to connect my physical body with my higher self. I want these energies to be working together, so I call a meeting! I sit with them and check in.

## Cleaning your aura

I think of every person I come into contact with as giving off a vibe, kind of like a wi-fi signal. Some have a strong signal, while others only have very low bars! Be aware of what your energy is like. Do an energy check before you leave the house, get out of the car or walk into a meeting or an event.

I have a sign on my office door that reads: 'Please be responsible for the energy that you are bringing into this room'. Our energy is more contagious than COVID-19! It blows me away that people will remove their dirty footwear before walking into a home or building but will not shake off their shitty energy.

Can you imagine how dirty your aura gets, bouncing around and bumping into other auras all day? In my perfect world, people would clean their auras as often as they clean their physical bodies! Regularly cleansing your energy field is a great habit to get into. You come into contact with loads of people and environments, all of which have their own energy vibrations, and not all of these frequencies are high and positive.

Cleaning your aura is easy. There are number of ways you can give your aura a clean and remove all the crap that you have collected throughout the day. Many of them involve water, which is a wonderful way to cleanse energy. Fresh bodies of water are made up of negative ions. Water can hold our intentions. It has always been used in spiritual rituals to cleanse and clear. Water is also very soothing. Symbolically, water represents your emotions and the unconscious mind. Therefore, just the sound of running water can promote a meditative state, as water works to smooth and soothe emotions.

## Swimming

A swim in the ocean, a plunge in a lake or a dip in a river will cleanse your aura. If you are not keen on swimming, just put your feet in and take a moment to imagine all your stress and tension washing away.

## Breathing

Several times a day, it is ideal to breathe. Well, we all need to breathe all day, but several times a day it is ideal if you can take two minutes and breathe *consciously*. Breathe deeply! Think of it as a quick clean-out. Inhale some life-enhancing air and energy, and exhale some bullshit. Keeping on top of this several times a day means you avoid a backlog of bullshit to deal with at the end of the day!

There are loads of special breathing techniques you can do that will drastically change your energy and shift your consciousness. Heart, diaphragmatic and alternate nostril breathing are all techniques that can change your physical, mental and spiritual state. Our lungs are such an important organ. It is wonderful to get into the habit of being aware of your breath. I do not remember breathing at all during the first 25 years of my life. I was always on the go, never slowing down long enough to notice my incredible lungs and all their great work.

I recently came across this poem from American poet John Roedel. It is so beautiful and speaks to how divine our lungs are. I was delighted when John gave me permission to share this in this book.

*my brain and*
*heart divorced*

*a decade ago*
*over who was*
*to blame about*
*how big of a mess*
*I have become*

*eventually,*
*they couldn't be*
*in the same room*
*with each other*

*now my head and heart*
*share custody of me*

*I stay with my brain*
*during the week*

*and my heart*
*gets me on weekends*

*they never speak to one another*
*– instead, they give me*
*– the same note to pass*
*– to each other every week*
*and their notes they*
*send to one another always*
*says the same thing:*

*"This is all your fault"*

*on Sundays*
*my heart complains*
*about how my*
*head has let me down*
*in the past*

*and on Wednesday*
*my head lists all*
*of the times my*
*heart has screwed*
*things up for me*
*in the future*

*they blame each*
*other for the*
*state of my life*

*there's been a lot*
*of yelling – and crying*

*so,*

*lately, I've been*
*spending a lot of*
*time with my gut*
*who serves as my*
*unofficial therapist*

*most nights, I sneak out of the*
*window in my ribcage*

*and slide down my spine*
*and collapse on my*
*gut's plush leather chair*
*that's always open for me*

*– and I just sit sit sit sit*
*until the sun comes up*

*last evening,*
*my gut asked me*
*if I was having a hard*
*time being caught*
*between my heart*
*and my head*

*I nodded*

*I said I didn't know*
*if I could live with*
*either of them anymore*

*"my heart is always sad about*
*something that happened yesterday*
*while my head is always worried*
*about something that may happen tomorrow,"*
*I lamented*

*my gut squeezed my hand*

*"I just can't live with*
*my mistakes of the past*
*or my anxiety about the future,"*
*I sighed*

*my gut smiled and said:*

*"in that case,*
*you should*
*go stay with your*
*lungs for a while,"*

*I was confused*
*– the look on my face gave it away*
*"if you are exhausted about*
*your heart's obsession with*
*the fixed past and your mind's focus*
*on the uncertain future*

*your lungs are the perfect place for you*

*there is no yesterday in your lungs*
*there is no tomorrow there either*

*there is only now*
*there is only inhale*
*there is only exhale*
*there is only this moment*

*there is only breath*

*and in that breath*
*you can rest while your*
*heart and head work*
*their relationship out."*

*this morning,*
*while my brain*
*was busy reading*
*tea leaves*

*and while my*
*heart was staring*
*at old photographs*

*I packed a little*
*bag and walked*
*to the door of*
*my lungs*

*before I could even knock*
*she opened the door*
*with a smile and as*
*a gust of air embraced me*
*she said*

*"what took you so long?"*

~ John Roedel

## Auric bathing

Laying in a bath of Epsom salts (magnesium sulphate) is a wonderful way to restore your physical body and cleanse your energetic self. I use one cup of Epsom salts and one cup of baking soda with some essential oils: lavender before bed and eucalyptus before an event.

## Spiritual showering

Stand in the shower and imagine the water is sparkly and silver. Feel it run all down you and visualise all bad energy, heavy situations and difficult people running down the drain! You can be commanding, saying out loud, 'I now remove all negative energy and entities from my field'.

## Smudging

You can use ancient herbs and sacred wood to cleanse your aura. Individual herbs or tied combinations can be used: dried sage for clearing negativity, cedar for new beginnings, rosemary for protection, sweet grass for clarity or palo santo for cleansing, spiritual healing. Circle the smoke of a smudge stick over your face with eyes closed, over your heart and limbs, over crown of your head and under your feet. You can also smudge rooms to clean energies, which is especially good after difficult conversations or arguments.

### Visualisation

Every night, when I get into bed, I do an energy scan of my body. I imagine a white wand circling my body scanning for anything dense or heavy. I ask my higher self if I have anything that needs clearing. I say, 'I release all negative energies, all energies that do not belong to me. I release all energies that are not for my highest good. I am love and light'.

If I have big things to remove, especially after an argument or a difficult day, I call in Archangel Michael. Archangel Michael is a leader and warrior in the angel world. He is the sexiest angel! He is very cool and powerful. He rides a motorbike and has a big sword! I ask him to 'make my aura anew – cut any cords and surround me in blue'.

## Clearing corded attachments

Cord cutting is a wonderful way to remove invisible ties between humans. I think of cords as vacuum-cleaner hoses running from one person to another. They bind us together at an energetic level. These 'cords' allow us to be wonderfully connected to people, and to send and receive messages to each other via intuition.

All of us have these cords – all of use create and receive them. The problem is with old cords that might no longer suit you. I remember when I first learnt about energetic cords. I couldn't unsee them! Suddenly, I was super aware of everyone and anyone that I might have had a cord connection with.

The cords are especially import when you are leaving jobs, relationships or locations, or if you are trying to change any part of your life. Cleaning up your cords can bring fresh energy and new opportunities.

There are several ways you can cut cords (see figure 4):

- **Meditation.** Ask your angels or guides to help you. Scan your body through your mind's eye and see where any cords might be attached. Ask your guides 'what instrument is required' to effectively remove each cord. I have used tiny embroidery scissors and huge machetes! Say out loud, 'Help me heal, let go, and cut any etheric cords that are no longer serving my higher purpose'.
- **Check before bed.** I like to check in each night before falling asleep. I ask my guides to remove any and all cords that are not aligned with my highest good and to surround me with loving light.
- **Paper cutting.** An excellent exercise I often do with clients is to draw two stick figures side by side. I get them to draw all the cords that they feel might be attached, naming each one: a cord of responsibility, a cord of financial dependence, a cord of social confidence. Once all the cords are identified, you cut the piece of paper in half with real scissors. Declare, 'I cut these ties with love and take back all my power'.

Figure 4: cutting the cord

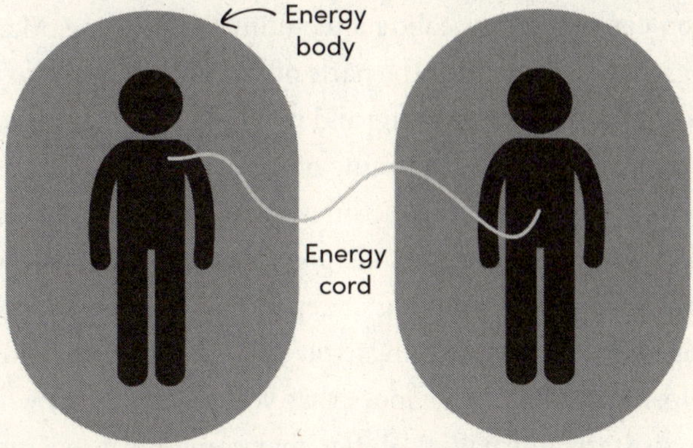


## Journalling

As you are exploring spirituality, get into the habit of journalling. Keep a journal of your thoughts and feelings. Write whatever comes to your mind. Use this journal as a tool of reflection, and it'll help you to better understand you.

Use your journal to write about what you notice, your thoughts and daily experiences. Notice people: who do you feel connected to? Who draws you in? Start to become aware of the energy around others. Follow your intuition about people, places and things you are connected to. You might feel connected to a certain lake, a town, a type of animal or a style of hat! All the things we are connected to give us clues to our soul's purpose, past and calling.

Also, notice yourself! Beneath the social mask we wear every day, we have a hidden self. This is often referred to as our 'shadow' – it's the self we really do not want to reveal to the world. It's the parts of us that we are not proud of and are often ashamed to admit to. There is so much gold in making friends with your shadow. Acknowledging the parts of yourself that you are not so keen on can be very revealing and, ultimately, healing. Many of us go to great lengths to hide the parts of ourselves that we do not like or are not proud of; examining and making peace with these bits of our personalities is the beginning of self-love.

Shadow work is a practice that helps us to regain access to our 'wholeness'; it works on the premise that you must own your shadow, rather than avoiding or repressing it, to experience deep healing. Writing lists of things you need to let go of, people you need to forgive and behaviours that you regret are all wonderful places to start. Journalling things that come up in everyday life, things that trigger memories or feelings and things that upset you is also worth doing regularly. Taking some time to write out what happened and how you felt, and when you have felt that way previously, will help you start to gather some awareness of some of your dark, shadowy bits!

*

Go to the next page to find ideas and suggestions to Get, Guard and Give spiritual energy.

# Getting spiritual energy is all about connection!

Your spiritual energy journey is yours. No one can tell you what to do or what practices to follow. It's definitely OK for you to ignore and block out other people's opinions (including mine) as they relate to your path. You might like to smudge your house, play with oracle cards or start praying. Just do what you feel is right for you. The most important thing is to remember to stay true and honest with yourself.

I am a huge advocate of always doing your own research, no matter the subject. Whether it be about your spiritual beliefs, old beliefs you've been taught or how to connect with your spiritual self, read books about different religions and spiritual practices, watch educational videos or movies, and talk to people to learn about their personal spiritual experiences. Ask all the questions! You will always be researching and learning on your spiritual journey.

Your journey is meant to help you grow, and you grow with knowledge and information. So, use your research, knowledge and personal experiences to form your own conclusions.

- **Connect to you:** Start a daily spiritual practice, such as meditation, visualisation or journalling, to connect with your higher self and understand your energy.
- **Take time:** Sit in stillness and create space for inner reflection and self-awareness. Use techniques such as energy scanning and visualisation to cleanse and balance your energy centres.
- **Collect wonderful people:** Being with people who you can be yourself with is very energising. Look for people who open you up, expand you and support you.

# Guarding spiritual energy is all about space!

We are here to take up space. We all need space to live well: physical space, emotional space, mental space and, most importantly, soul space. To grow, a plant needs space; we are the same. Mediating gives your head space. Creating a sacred space dedicated to your spiritual energy is an excellent way to honour your soul self.

There are many energy-guarding techniques that you can use in different situations. If you know you are going to a big event or a difficult meeting, you can use 'the zipper': you can zip yourself up, starting at the groin and using your hand as if you are zipping up a large hoodie that goes all the way up over your head, and say, 'I am safe from all negative and unhelpful energies'. Another technique that is perfect when you are dashing around and not expecting to bump into difficult or heavy people is to pretend that you have a garage door opener in your hand. Press the imaginary button and imagine a crystal-clear glass door coming down between you and the person you are interacting with, shielding you from their energy and any other shit!

When you start to grow and step into new areas of interest, you might find that as your mind expands, the number of people you have in your world shrinks! Like a snake shedding a skin, you will find that you shed ideas, items and people in your growth. I have found that every time I have levelled up my life, I have lost people. It's not a bad thing. Some people may be threatened by your new interests or energy. Some people will no longer hold your interest. You find yourself less interested in their conversation and less concerned about the things they are concerned about. You are literally vibrating on a different wavelength. People either disappear or you will wish that they would!

Often, evolving requires elimination. When you are committed to evolving, to improving and expanding your consciousness, people who are committed to revolving rather than evolving will disappear. People find change very scary. When you change, they will be nervous. You growing may not suit them! Sometimes, to create, we must be willing to destroy. Let them go. Bless them and release them. Mentally thank them for who and what they have been in your world, but know that letting them go is part of your growth.

- **Create a space:** Create space physically for yourself. Having a space where you are surrounded by things that you love is good for your soul. It might be a favourite chair, a few cushions, a sacred altar or a whole room – somewhere for you to do you.
- **Set boundaries:** Protect your energy by using shielding techniques to protect yourself in challenging situations. Remove yourself from physical places that you do not feel OK in.
- **Let go and grow:** Understand that growth may require letting go of people or beliefs that no longer align with your spiritual journey.

## Giving spiritual energy is all about love!

As Neale Donald Walsch explains it, 'Ultimately, all thoughts are sponsored by love or fear. All thoughts, ideas, concepts, understandings, decisions, choices, and actions are based on these. And, in the end, there is really only one. Love. In truth, love is all there is'.

- **Choose love over fear:** Choose love in your thoughts, actions and interactions with others and yourself.
- **Practise self-love, self-forgiveness and self-acceptance:** Radiate positive energy.
- **Contribute to the collective consciousness:** Embrace love, empathy, and kindness in your interactions with the world. Recognise the interconnectedness of all energy fields and how your energy can influence the world around you.

These actions encompass a holistic approach to managing and enhancing your energy, fostering self-awareness and contributing positively to both your own well-being and the broader collective consciousness.

# APPENDIX: THE SEVEN CHAKRAS

## 1. Root or base chakra

- **Location:** Base of spine
- **Element:** Earth
- **Qualities:** Safety, courage and stability
- **Colour:** Red
- **Affirmation:** I am present and aware
- **Ability:** To be
- **Governs:** Trust and fear
- **Deals with:** Survival
- **Blocked by:** Fear
- **When energised:** Grounded, prosperous and calm
- **When off:** Insecure, materialistic, prone to overspending and hoarding
- **Physical, mental and emotional issues:** Depression, addiction and issues with lower back, legs, bowels and feet
- **Actions:** Examine beliefs and superstitions. Walk barefoot. Sit on the floor. Spend time gardening.
- **Notes:** Feeling very materialistic or insecure about what other people have can be a sign that this chakra is out of whack.

## 2. Sacral chakra

- **Location:** Below the belly button
- **Element:** Water
- **Qualities:** Creativity, pleasure and sexuality
- **Colour:** Orange
- **Affirmation:** I am creative/productive
- **Ability:** To feel
- **Governs:** Connection and feelings
- **Deals with:** Pleasure
- **Blocked by:** Guilt
- **When energised:** Graceful, nurturing and passionate
- **When off:** Emotional, possessing low self-esteem
- **Physical, mental and emotional issues:** Issues with stomach or bladder, hips, sex organs and gallstones
- **Actions:** Be creative. Get comfortable with your sexuality. Swim or have a warm bath. Listen to water sounds.
- **Notes:** If you are feeling misunderstood, lonely and emotional for no apparent reason, this can be a sign that your sacral chakra is blocked or sluggish.

## 3. Solar plexus chakra

- **Location:** Above the belly button
- **Element:** Fire
- **Qualities:** Strength, confidence and determination
- **Colour:** Yellow
- **Affirmation:** I create my own reality
- **Ability:** To act
- **Governs:** Personal power and proactivity
- **Deals with:** Willpower
- **Blocked by:** Shame
- **When energised:** Warm, spontaneous and disciplined
- **When off:** Spontaneous, disciplined and emotionally warm
- **Physical, mental and emotional issues:** Eating disorders, ulcers and issues with stomach, digestive system, liver, kidneys and pancreas
- **Actions:** Work on being less critical and more loving towards yourself and others. Spend time in the sun or sauna. Fast for 24 hours. Light candles.
- **Notes:** I get very critical of everything and everyone – bordering on aggressive – when my solar plexus chakra is out.

## 4. Heart chakra

- **Location:** Centre of chest
- **Element:** Air
- **Qualities:** Forgiving, caring and acceptance
- **Colour:** Green
- **Affirmation:** I welcome experiences that help me grow
- **Ability:** To love
- **Governs:** Love and harmony
- **Deals with:** Love
- **Blocked by:** Grief
- **When energised:** Kind, peaceful and empathetic
- **When off:** Jealous, people-pleasing and lonely
- **Physical, mental and emotional issues:** Sadness, trouble breathing, weak immune system and issues with chest, lungs, heart, shoulders and breast
- **Actions:** Seek emotional healing and healing in relationships. Wear green. Spend time with animals. Practise gratitude. Work on the balance in your life: give/get, work/home, masculine/feminine
- **Notes:** Making passive aggressive comments and feeling hopeless are always signs for me that my heart chakra needs some love.

## 5. Throat chakra

- **Location:** Neck
- **Element:** Sound
- **Qualities:** Creativity and expressivity
- **Colour:** Blue
- **Affirmation:** I express my truth
- **Ability:** To speak
- **Governs:** Communication, connection and expression
- **Deals with:** Truth
- **Blocked by:** Lies
- **When energised:** Inspired, honest and patient
- **When off:** Afraid of speaking your truth but gossipy about others
- **Physical, mental and emotional issues:** Secrets, trouble communicating, arguing and issues with throat, ears, neck, thyroid, jaw and teeth
- **Actions:** Work on control issues by learning to go with the flow. Read poetry. Listen to music. Sing.
- **Notes:** Many women have trouble with their throat chakra. They often do not feel listened to or able to make decisions for themselves. They feel like they have no power in their lives, so they become controlling and passive aggressive! Trying to control everyone is exhausting.

## 6. Brow chakra

- **Location:** Between the eyebrows
- **Element:** Light
- **Qualities:** Imagination and perception
- **Colour:** Purple
- **Affirmation:** I let go of all my limiting beliefs
- **Ability:** To see
- **Governs:** Awareness and wisdom
- **Deals with:** Insight
- **Blocked by:** Illusion
- **When energised:** Visionary, imaginative and intuitive
- **When off:** Sceptical, insensitive and obsessive
- **Physical, mental and emotional issues:** Headaches, migraines, insomnia and issues with brain, eyes, nose and pituitary gland
- **Actions:** Be positive. Check your attitude. Wear purple or indigo. Meditate. Draw or colour in.
- **Notes:** I notice when my brow chakra is off as I get very rigid! I become judgemental and hard to be around.

## 7. Crown chakra

- **Location:** Top of the head
- **Element:** Spirit
- **Qualities:** Spiritual insight
- **Colour:** White
- **Affirmation:** I want to learn
- **Ability:** To know
- **Governs:** Consciousness and spirituality
- **Deals with:** Cosmic energy
- **Blocked by:** Ego attachment
- **When energised:** Present, open and masterful
- **When off:** Judgemental, confused and suffering brain fog or closed-mindedness
- **Physical, mental and emotional issues:** Loneliness, depression and issues with bones, skin and nervous system
- **Actions:** Learn to be grateful and guided. Have faith! Journal. Rest. Spend time in nature.
- **Notes:** When you are disconnected from yourself and those around you, you will feel sensitive, needy and possibly depressed.

# ABOUT THE AUTHOR

Lisa O'Neill is a keynote speaker, business mentor and author with over 20 years of experience making people and organisations better! She is passionate about helping people take charge of their energy and live lives that they love. Lisa is consistently top-rated in conference and event evaluations. She has the unique ability to deliver heavy messages in a light and relatable way, and participants love her straight-talking, refreshing wisdom and infectious laughter.

Lisa has written seven books on topics such as self-love, happiness, chaos, action and energy. She loves experience design, tailoring her messages to suit audiences, industries and conference themes. Lisa is guaranteed to leave you inspired, energised and ready to change the way you think about life.

Listen to Lisa's podcast *Offstage with Lisa O'Neill* at:
lisaoneill.co.nz/podcast

# REFERENCES


## Chapter 1

Hay, L, *You Can Heal Your Life*, Hay House, 1984.

## Chapter 2

*Oxford English Dictionary*, s.v., 'awe (n.1)', July 2023, <oed.com/dictionary/awe_n1>.

Hollie Holden - Notes on Living & Loving, Facebook post, 17 January 2019, <facebook.com/hollieholdenlove/photos/a.652449231538953/1968882349895628>.

Akhondi, H & Ross, AB, *Gluten-associated Medical Problems*, StatPearls Publishing, 2024.

Ford, RPK, 'The gluten syndrome: a neurological disease', *Medical Hypotheses*, vol. 73, no. 3, 2009, pp. 438–440.

Schreier, HMC & Wright, RJ, 'Stress and food allergy: mechanistic considerations', *Annals of Allergy, Asthma & Immunology*, vol. 112, no. 4, 2013, pp. 296–301.

Buret, AG, 'How stress induces intestinal hypersensitivity', *The American Journal of Pathology*, vol. 168, no. 1, 2006, pp. 3–5.

Harvard Health Publishing, 'Know the facts about fats', blog post, Harvard Medical School, 19 April 2021, <health.harvard.edu/staying-healthy/know-the-facts-about-fats>.

St. Pierre, B, 'Every question about PN's hand-portion method—answered.', Precision Nutrition, accessed 4 March 2024, <precisionnutrition.com/hand-portion-faq>.

Kleiner, SM, 'Water: an essential but overlooked nutrient', *Journal of the American Dietetic Association*, vol. 99, no. 2, 1999, pp. 200–206.

Chen, J, Jayachandran, M, Bai, W & Xu, B, 'A critical review on the health benefits of fish consumption and its bioactive constituents', *Food Chemistry*, vol. 369, 2022, e130874.

Rana, A et al., 'Health benefits of polyphenols: a concise review', *Journal of Food Biochemistry*, vol. 46, no. 10, 2022, e14264.

Cömert, ED, Mogol, BA & Gökmen, V, 'Relationship between color and antioxidant capacity of fruits and vegetables', *Current Research in Food Science*, vol. 21, no. 2, 2019, pp. 1–10.

Brodie, K, *An Invitation To Rest | He Tono Kia Okioki*, self-published, n.d.

Mah, J & Pitre, T, 'Oral magnesium supplementation for insomnia in older adults: a systematic review & meta-analysis', *BMC Complementary Medicine and Therapies*, vol. 21, no. 1, 2021, p. 125.

Lee, Y-C, Lu, C-T, Cheng, W-N & Li, H-Y, 'The impact of mouth-taping in mouth-breathers with mild obstructive sleep apnea: a preliminary study', *Healthcare* (Basel, Switzerland), vol. 10, no. 9, 2022, p. 1755.

Stassinopoulos Huffington, A, *The Sleep Revolution: Transforming your life, one night at a time*, Harmony Books, 2016.

Saint-Maurice, PF et al., 'Estimated number of deaths prevented through increased physical activity among US adults', *JAMA Internal Medicine*, vol. 182, no. 3, 2022, pp. 349–352.

Williams, C, *Move: The new science of body over mind*, Profile Books, 2021.

Roth, G, *Sweat Your Prayers*, Penguin, 1997.

Fogg, BJ, *Tiny Habits*, Random House, 2019.

Henry, T, *Die Empty*, Penguin, 2013.

## Chapter 3

Mcleod, S, 'Maslow's hierarchy of needs', *Simply Psychology*, updated 24 January 2024, <simplypsychology.org/maslow.html>.

*Inside out*, motion picture, Walt Disney Studios Motion Pictures, 2015.

Paul Ekman Group, 'Micro expressions', accessed 4 March 2024, <paulekman.com/micro-expressions/>.

Cretsinger, MM, 'Understanding the mind-body connection for optimal health and healing', *Graduate Research Papers*, 2006, 379.

Hawkins, DR, *The Map of Consciousness Explained: A proven energy scale to actualize your ultimate potential*, Hay House, 2020.

Singer, MA, *The Untethered Soul: The journey beyond yourself*, ReadHowYouWant.com, 2009.

*The Fault in Our Stars*, motion picture, Fox 2000 Pictures, 2014.

McLaren, K, *Emotional Vocabulary List*, self-published, n.d.

Han, S, 'You can only maintain so many close friendships', *The Atlantic*, 20 May 2021, <theatlantic.com/family/archive/2021/05/robin-dunbar-explains-circles-friendship-dunbars-number/618931/>.

*World's Greatest Dad*, motion picture, Magnolia Pictures, 2009.

Klue, L, *52 Conversations: Looking at life from around the corner*, self-published, n.d.

Latta, N, *The Politically Incorrect Guide to Teenagers*, HarperCollins Australia, 2011.

O'Neill, L, *The Lickable Third*, self-published, 2018.

Morris, NW, *Your 33 Day Money Action Plan: How to get out of debt, save money, discover financial peace, and revolutionize your view of money forever*, CreateSpace Independent Publishing Platform, 2012.

Marianne Williamson, X (Twitter) post, 15 August 2017, 7.20 p.m., <twitter.com/marwilliamson/status/897387483524157440>.

House, O, *The Invitation*, HarperONE, San Francisco, 1999.

O'Neill, L, *Look Gorgeous, Be Happy*, Penguin, 2013.

## Chapter 4

Ballmann, CG, 'The influence of music performance on exercise responses and performance: a review', *Journal of Functional Morphology and Kinesiology*, vol. 6, no. 2, 2021, p. 33.

Marshall, L, 'Suicide rates in the US are on the rise: New study offers surprising reasons why', *CU Boulder Today*, 15 February 2024, <colorado.edu/today/2024/02/15/suicide-rates-us-are-rise-new-study-offers-surprising-reasons-why>.

Kresovich, A, 'The influence of pop songs referencing anxiety, depression, and suicidal ideation on college students' mental health empathy, stigma, and behavioral intentions', *Health Communication*, vol. 37, no. 5, 2022, pp. 617–627.

Clear, J, *Atomic Habits: Tiny changes, remarkable results: an easy and proven way to build good habits and break bad ones*, Avery, 2018.

Katie, B, *Loving What Love Is*, Rider, 2002.

Helder, C, *Useful Belief*, John Wiley & Sons, 2015.

Williamson, M, *A Return to Love*, HarperCollins, 1992.

Covey, SR, *The 7 Habits of Highly Effective People: Restoring the character ethic*, Simon and Schuster, 1989.

Gibran, K, *The Prophet*, Alfred A. Knopf, 1923.

O'Neill, L, *Everything YOU Want*, self-published, 2020.

## Chapter 5

International Network for the Study of Spirituality, 'Spirituality and Consciousness Studies (SaCS) SIG', accessed 4 March 2024, <spiritualitystudiesnetwork.org/Spirituality-and-Consciousness-Studies-SIG>.

Miller, K, 'Science of spirituality (+16 ways to become more spiritual)', *PositivePsychology.com*, 16 April 2020, <positivepsychology.com/science-of-spirituality/>.

Spencer, M, 'What is spirituality? A personal exploration', Royal College of Psychiatrists, accessed 4 March 2024, <rcpsych.ac.uk/docs/default-source/members/sigs/spirituality-spsig/what-is-spirituality-maya-spencer-x.pdf>.

Brown, B, *The Gifts of Imperfection: Let go of who you think you're supposed to be and embrace who you are*, Hazelden Publishing, 2010.

Oliver, M, 'The Summer Day', poem, *New and Selected Poems*, Beacon Press, 1992.

# RECOMMENDED READING LIST

***Be Happy! Release the power of happiness in YOU*, by Robert Holden (Hay House, 2009)**

Learn about true happiness, who you really are and what your life is for. Robert teaches happiness techniques, principles and insights that will help you to embrace happiness at a deep level.

***Big Magic: Creative living beyond fear*, by Elizabeth Gilbert (Penguin, 2015)**

I love Liz Gilbert's unique understanding of creativity. This book will change the way you think and live! It will make you curious and help you to embrace ideas and creative thinking.

***The Body is the Barometer of the Soul: So be your own doctor*, by Annette Noontil (self-published, 1994)**

This book shows you the simple way to change your thoughts to change your body. Discover how the body reacts to your thoughts and situations and how to change negatives into healthy positives.

***Breath: The new science of a lost art*, by James Nestor (Riverhead Books, 2020)**

This book is a game changer. Breathing is the most important thing that we do, and yet we do not understand how to do it properly. *Breath* turns on its head the conventional wisdom of what we thought we knew about our most basic biological function. You will never breathe the same again.

***Conversations with God: An uncommon dialogue (Book 1),* by Neale Donald Walsch (G.P. Putnam's Sons, 1996)**

This excellent book is about an unemployed homeless man who becomes an 'accidental spiritual messenger'. Loaded with questions and answers from 'god', this book changed my relationship with the word 'god'.

***Faster Than Normal: Turbocharge your focus, productivity, and success with the secrets of the ADHD brain,* by Peter Shankman (Penguin, 2017)**

This is an amazing book for anyone with ADHD. It contains strategies for working with a brain that often goes way too fast!

***The Four Agreements: A practical guide to personal freedom,* by Don Miguel Ruiz (Amber-Allen Publishing, 1997)**

This is an easy book to read It contains four easy concepts that you can use immediately to free your thinking and change the way you live every day!

***The Gifts of Imperfection: Let go of who you think you're supposed to be and embrace who you are,* by Brené Brown (Hazelden Publishing, 2010)**

One of Brené's early books, this book is great for anyone who needs to step out of who they think they have to be and into who they really are. It is the perfect book for helping you feel worthy and whole!

***I Thought It Was Just Me (But It Isn't),* by Brené Brown (Penguin, 2007)**

This is the perfect book for anyone who suffers from perfectionism. It will help with the exhaustion of social expectations and feeling inadequate.

***The Instruction: Living the life your soul intended,* by Ainslie MacLeod (Sounds True, 2007)**

Ainslie is a psychic who teaches about spirit guides and the impact that past lives have on our current lives. This is an excellent book on identifying your soul purpose, soul type and soul age.

***The Invitation*, by Oriah Mountain Dreamer (Element, 2000)**

A world-famous poem broken down into chapters, *The Invitation* helped me to understand what's really important in life, as well as the concept of self-betrayal! It still gives me goosebumps every time I read it.

***The Last Lecture*, by Jeffrey Zaslow and Randy Pausch (Hyperion, 2008)**

This is a terminally ill college professor›s last speech to his students in book form. Containing lessons in living, it is a life-changing book that helps you get perspective around what really matters.

***Life Is Short, Wear Your Party Pants*, by Loretta LaRoche (Hay House, 2003)**

Filled with joy and laughter, this book is loaded with solid, practical ways to slow down, reconnect with what matters and celebrate yourself. It is an excellent book for anyone who is overly responsible and needs permission to have more fun!

***Living Untethered: Beyond the human predicament*, by Michael A Singer (New Harbinger Publications, 2022)**

This incredible book teaches us to look inside for real freedom, love and inspiration. This book helped me to discover a deeper understanding my emotions, where my thoughts and moods come from and how to embrace my natural energy flow.

***A Return to Love: Reflections on the principles of a course in miracles*, by Marianne Williamson (HarperCollins, 1992)**

This book contains, reflections and insights on the application and expression of love in your daily life. Marianne Williamson uses very Christian language, but her writing is beautiful.

***Sacred Contracts: Awakening your divine potential*, by Caroline Myss (Random House, 2001)**

I love the idea of knowing the sacred contracts that we have signed up for. This book helps us live in alignment with our spiritual commitments.

***The Secret Language of the Body*, by Inna Segal (Blue Angel Gallery, 2007)**

This powerful handbook helps us to understand the messages our body sends us and the underlying energetic causes. It›s my go-to for any ailments that my body has.

***Seven Spiritual Laws of Success: A practical guide to the fulfillment of your dreams*, by Deepak Chopra (Amber-Allen Publishing, 1994)**

Learn to take responsibility for your life. This wee book is filled with harmony, fulfilment, abundance and advice for living effortlessly.

***There›s a Spiritual Solution to Every Problem*, by Wayne Dyer (HarperCollins, 2001)**

We often look to our intellect to solve our problems. Wayne Dyer shows us that we can use spiritual energy for problem-solving. This a book about self-awareness and tapping into the healing energy within all of us.

***Tune In: Let your intuition guide you to fulfillment and flow*, by Sonia Choquette (Hay House, 2013)**

Learn to trust your vibes and follow your instincts with this guide to using your intuition.

***Why People Don't Heal and How They Can*, by Caroline Myss (Harmony, 1998)**

A practical approach to healing, Caroline teaches how to overcome the mental and emotional blocks to becoming well, and how to reconnect with an inner and outer spiritual energy and purpose.

***You Can Heal Your Life*, by Louise Hay (Hay House, 1984)**

This book is a game changer for taking responsibility for your life. Louise Hay has had the most impact on my life of all the teachers whose work I have studied. The power of affirmations to change our programming and the connection that our minds have with our bodies are the two biggest learnings.

# CONTACT LISA

I am obsessed with inspiring action and helping people get out of their own way: liberating humans from beliefs and self-imposed limits that no longer serve them, and designing lives and business solutions that change the way people think.

To inquire about retreats, events, leadership programs, mentoring and keynotes, please email **hello@lisaoneill.co.nz** or visit **lisaoneill.co.nz**.